CW00348729

HALLELUJAH FOR 50ft WOMEN

HALLELUJAH FOR 50ft WOMEN

POEMS ABOUT WOMEN'S RELATIONSHIP TO THEIR BODIES

EDITED BY RAVING BEAUTIES

BLOODAXE BOOKS

Selection and introduction copyright © 2015 Raving Beauties

Copyright of poems rests with authors and other rights
holders as cited in the acknowledgements on pages 169-172,
which constitute an extension of this copyright page.

ISBN: 978 1 78037 155 9

First published 2015 by
Bloodaxe Books Ltd,
Eastburn,
South Park,
Hexham,
Northumberland NE46 1BS.

www.bloodaxebooks.com
For further information about Bloodaxe titles
please visit our website or write to
the above address for a catalogue.

Supported by
ARTS COUNCIL
ENGLAND

LEGAL NOTICE

All rights reserved. No part of this book may be reproduced,
stored in a retrieval system, or transmitted in any form, or
by any means, electronic, mechanical, photocopying,
recording or otherwise, without prior written permission
from the copyright holders listed on pages 169-172.

Bloodaxe Books Ltd only controls publication rights to
poems from its own publications and does *not* control
rights to most of the poems published in this anthology.

The right of Raving Beauties to be identified as Editors
of this work has been asserted by them in accordance with
the Copyright, Designs and Patents Act 1988.

Printed in Great Britain by Bell & Bain Limited, Glasgow, Scotland, on
acid-free paper sourced from mills with FSC chain of custody certification.

CONTENTS

INTRODUCTION

You think you're doing it for someone else but it's never the whole story is it? This collection of poetry written by women with intelligence, grace, wit and honesty is for you Dear Reader. But it's also for us, Dee, Sue and Fan, another adventure to stop us from falling into the deep sleep of fairy tales where we can still dream of perfection and rescuers, shape changers who will bring us to the happy ever after ending. Let us pinch ourselves. Hard.

When Raving Beauties were performing and publishing poetry anthologies with The Women's Press in the 1980s we were still enmeshed in very personal struggles to achieve a utilitarian sanity which would bring personal and professional balance into our lives. It's been a long, rich road.

When we first addressed our desire to work together again a year or two ago we thought we'd look back over the thirty years (impossible!) that have passed since our first cabaret *In the Pink* and spend some time examining the changes, improvements and growth in women's lives. How could we not have flourished, we had worked so hard on ourselves, on nurturing our children, our jobs, our relationships, our precious creativity, our souls?

But somehow that task was too huge – a work of prose perhaps not poetry. So instead we decided to focus on an area where there was still trouble enough. A place where abuse, commerce, politics, time, culture and religion still have their battleground – our bodies. When will Eve ever be naked and sinless?

In the preface to *In the Pink*, Fan wrote 'We cannot *exchange* womanhood for personhood. Breast and cunt endure. We must go into the beauty of womanhood, not get out of it.' And here are wonderful hymns to breast, cunt and blood. Yeah baby. There are also poems about surviving, hate, vulnerability, witnessing, lust, dresses, gender, violence, oppression, chocolate, fat, coughing, ageing, death, teeth, mermaids, shaving, mirrors, rock 'n' roll, getting your feet done, earth and sky. And many, many more.

Hallelujah for 50ft Women has been selected from over a thousand submissions as well as previously published poetry. Every poet and poem has contributed to its vitality. We hope it draws us together, reminding us yet again that more binds us than divides us. The power of poetic language as the magic tool in this enterprise, used with all the skills, integrity and experience at our poets' command, is most precious. In the beginning was the word. And words belong to everyone.

Free but not cheap.

May we, in Heidi Williamson's words, 'ride the day' together.

And finally we'd like to mention two 50ft women in particular – Alexandra Viner and Karen Evans – thank you.

SUE, DEE & FAN

Horse

I've never seen a soul detached from its gender,
but I'd like to. I'd like to see my own that way,
free of its female tethers. Maybe it would be like
riding a horse. The rider's the human one,
but everyone looks at the horse.

CHASE TWICHELL

Genetics

My father's in my fingers, but my mother's in my palms.
I lift them up and look at them with pleasure –
I know my parents made me by my hands.

They may have been repelled to separate lands,
to separate hemispheres, may sleep with other lovers,
but in me they touch where fingers link to palms.

With nothing left of their togetherness but friends
who quarry for their image by a river,
at least I know their marriage by my hands.

I shape a chapel where a steeple stands.
And when I turn it over,
my father's by my fingers, my mother's by my palms

demure before a priest reciting psalms.
My body is their marriage register.
I re-enact their wedding with my hands.

So take me with you, take up the skin's demands
for mirroring in bodies of the future.
I'll bequeath my fingers, if you bequeath your palms.
We know our parents make us by our hands.

SINÉAD MORRISSEY

In Praise of My Legs:

Pillars. Scissors. Solid to their middles,
sticks of rock, printed with my mother's
maiden name, Edwards – *Potatoes* –
playground chant sung for
knobbly knees, skipperty wickets,
rickety from rickets – *she was raised*
in a sweet shop – fed on jars of
licorice allsorts and sherbet lemons.
I have my mother's laugh
and my mother's legs –
they have their flaws:
tiled, carpeted,
lino, paved.
Boughs, beams,
turned, shaped.
My legs run like ship-masts,
lift up the sails of my hips
to fall from the crest
of their iliac wave,
noble as whale bones,
sheer as cliffs,
walk me strident,
drumstick defiant
to the shops,
to the park,
to the pub

through the rain,
candy-striped
and white with sun
flashing   brilliant,
run, dance, bend
through the hours,
days, weeks,
years.
My mother.
My mother.
My legs.

Amen.

LYDIA TOWSEY

The Magic of the Foot

*Think of the magic of that foot, comparatively small, upon
which your whole weight rests. It's a miracle, and the dance
is a celebration of that miracle.*

MARTHA GRAHAM

After
when your body
no longer belongs to you
when it's still out there
in last night's darkness
seeking its way
into the sublime
those tendril feet
licking against the spine
of the stage,
After the lights
and the thrum of applause

15

have lifted into the streets
and slipped
into strangers' apartments
to live between wall hangings
and philosophy books
like remnants,
After all this
don't be surprised
to find yourself
in the same position again
splayed out on the bedroom floor
legs prised open
like a jewel box
the hinges
singing odes to joy
and the feet
those tiny miracles
pushing up and around
until they are joined
like hands
meeting wildly
unforgettably.

TISHANI DOSHI

Wearing Sexuality

There are ocelot coats in dusty wardrobes
reeking of ancient amber perfume the kind formulated
from rare creatures musk: borrowed hormones

There are these skins belonging to adults
an air of naked flesh and fur
the pelt of an adult woman

It only figures in the mind later
this habit of men buying women
these exotic skins hoping to see more skin

more shorn skin carefully defurred
skin prepped for a scene to be conducted
as under a low cloud

and you are to be left deflated
he has taken your breath with his promises
and you are left anxiously, animalistically,

sniffing your crotch surreptitiously
for that familiar ore scent
the smell of blood

ANNA PERCY

The Mermaid in the dime museum

As her village recedes to a distant speck,
she unpicks a loose stitch on the passenger seat. Her new boyfriend
turns, assures her of the wonderful life
waiting in the West. With her talent, she can easily
make it as a dancer. This will be her fortune.

> *A Japanese fisherman sits by the receding tide,*
> *sewing. Stitches smaller than rice grains*
> *seamlessly blend scales and fur.*
> *His finger tips trace the tail's sensuous curve.*
> *He smiles. This will be his fortune.*

Hair extensions; Brazilian; spray tan; acrylic nails.
She's worried about the cost, but her boyfriend doesn't hesitate,
hands his credit card over. As she leaves the salon
she sees Venus reflected in the glass:
new born, radiant, shawled in ocean mist.

> *The sum is more than five bolts of silk,*
> *but the Dutch merchant doesn't hesitate,*
> *pays the Japanese fisherman, wraps it in a shawl*
> *and carries it, tenderly as a newborn,*
> *up the gangplank.*

She wonders why her dance audition is in a hotel,
but her boyfriend tells her to shut the fuck up, stop asking questions.
The receptionist is indifferent; he's seen it all,
leads her through labyrinthine corridors to a plain white room.
The director looks her up and down; tells her to undress.

> *In an alley among whores, drunks and the stench of fish,*
> *the Dutch merchant strikes a bargain with an American captain,*
> *who has to sell his ship. Years later, broke, he sells the mermaid*
> *for a fraction of what he paid. But that's the way with sirens,*
> *bestowing fortune or grief as whim dictates.*

Bathed in his laptop's subaqueous glow,
a man wanders the internet's dark alleys, safe search off.
He finds a video of a girl with buoyant breasts
and hairless sex sprawled on the bed
of a white hotel room. He clicks.

> *The posters appear overnight: a genuine mermaid,*
> *caught off the shores of distant 'Feejee'. Crowds surge*
> *to the museum, pay their dime. The men go to catch a glimpse*
> *of milky skin, flowing hair, peeping nipples;*
> *the women to hear the songs she must surely sing.*

She dies several times a day; fakes so many little deaths
she's starting to feel a part of her has died inside.
By now she doesn't have to think: just curls her lips,
and, eyes glassy, looks at the wave-like patterns on the ceiling
while her co-star fills the red-pink shell of her sex.

Munching popcorn and cotton candy, the punters
walk past waxworks of famous murderers, but still are not prepared
for the sight of a blackened baby orang-utan with a salmon tail.
The Feejee Mermaid sprawls in its case,
glass eyes reflecting all those drowned expressions,
lips curled as though in laughter at some secret joke.

ALEX TOMS

Her Mother Hides in the Wardrobe

Julia wears a pink dress and earrings,
has green eyes and a pony tail.
She has herpes, hepatitis, thrush,
staphylococcus, cervical erosion, HIV.

She lives with her mum and dad in
a studio flat in an old district of Kiev.
They have three cats: Hanka, Efedra,
Morifius – opium, ephedrine, morphine.

She learns English before Euro 2012;
'my name is Julia, fifty dollars fifty minutes'.

BOGUSIA WARDIEN

Katie's end of week routine

Ah step, tenderly
into a small ocean.
Lower each inch
of skin

in nobody's eyes.
A layer of lavender
bubbles. No need
for acting

ah let ma belly hang
its childbearin'
rounded pear shape.
Drop ma whole body

in. Caressed by heat
of the water. Protected,
enveloped, like a baby
in its mother's womb

listening to the rhythm
of ma heartbeat as ah once
did hers. Ah submerge
ma head, float

until ah surface,
gaspin' for breath.
Washin' their hands,
their eyes away

from memory.
Emerge skin pink,
soft, fresh as
a newborn.

JULIE EDGELL

Three Ways of Recovering a Body

By chance I was alone in my bed the morning
I woke to find my body had gone.
It had been coming. I'd cut off my hair in sections
so each of you would have something to remember,
then my nails worked loose from their beds
of oystery flesh. Who was it got them?
One night I slipped out of my skin. It lolloped
hooked to my heels, hurting. I had to spray on
more scent so you could find me in the dark,
I was going so fast. One of you begged for my ears
because you could hear the sea in them.

First I planned to steal myself back. I was a mist
on thighs, belly and hips. I'd slept with so many men.
I was with you in the ash-haunted stations of Poland,
I was with you on that grey plaza in Berlin
while you wolfed three doughnuts without stopping,
thinking yourself alone. Soon I recovered my lips
by waiting behind the mirror while you shaved.
You pouted. I peeled away kisses like wax
no longer warm to the touch. Then I flew off.

Next I decided to become a virgin. Without a body
it was easy to make up a new story. In seven years
every invisible cell would be renewed
and none of them would have touched any of you.
I went to a cold lake, to a grey-lichened island,
I was gold in the wallet of the water.
I was known to the inhabitants, who were in love
with the coveted whisper of my virginity:
all too soon they were bringing me coffee and perfume,
cash under stones. I could really do something for them.

Thirdly I tried marriage to a good husband
who knew my past but forgave it. I believed in the power
of his penis to smoke out all those men
so that bit by bit my body service would resume,

although for a while I'd be the one woman in the world
who was only present in the smile of her vagina.
He stroked the air where I might have been.
I turned to the mirror and saw mist gather
as if someone lived in the glass. Recovering
I breathed to myself, *'Hold on! I'm coming.'*

HELEN DUNMORE

Grandmother

My Grandmother's shoes are laced-up tight
beneath her dress of stretched violet.
Her jars of beans are counted and polished,
her starched, bleached sheets hung out to dry.

Streuth, girl, she says, when a man beats you
it's with the beam of love in his eye.
I'll choose for you a man made of meat –
if he feeds you, he'll feed you the best cuts of the beast.

Here come the men like a full river,
here the men come like a rope, thrown.
They bring their gifts of broken-legged horses,
ready-made cigarettes and pressure pans.

They talk to Grandmother in her breathless kitchen,
as she skims the cream or stirs the tub.
They talk to Grandmother in the ticking parlour
where she rocks and rocks a creaking pram.

If they put their knuckles or flesh against me,
I'll kick the parlour chairs, I'll break their hands.
You can shut me up in the oasthouse, Grandmother,
my neck will be snow-smirred, scalded with ice.

22

I may be gloved and small-footed, Grandma,
I may seem, in my black dress, all shy of the plough;
but my empty bowl gleams like a chosen thing
and my heart, Grandma, my heart is a field.

SUZANNE BATTY

Ventriloquist

In life your anger never burned in words,
You turned away and whispered as you went
To clean or cook; that sibilance we heard
As if from some small dying creature sent.

You spoke in polished ornaments and flowers
Arranged in vases, pastry made for pies,
In floors scrubbed clean and whites you boiled for hours.
One morning woke and knew that these were lies.

In search of truth wherever it might be,
You followed all those unsaid words you'd thrown
Down to the beach, and straight into the sea,
Your apron on, its pockets full of stone.

Looking for you, feet sinking in the sands,
I see white death with fish held in her hands.

RUTH AYLETT

Bright Day

(i.m. my mother)

There is a sea of people
in the church. The ceilings are high.
I have made the long walk
to the golden railings on my spindly legs
in my white Communion shoes and socks.
The crowd pushes to the big swing doors.
Outside it's a bright, bright day.
The white sun flashes at me and I want
to fall, the cough I was keeping
at the back of my throat starts to bark.
My mother looks at me, at my white face,
at the black rings circling my eyes.
She has a question on her face.
She stretches out her arm, her hand
cups my elbow, her other hand clasps
my wrist – helping me across the road.
The sun's daggers are flicking
at cars as they pass. My spiky elbow
rests in my mother's cupped hand
in the soft pads. Her roly-poly fingers
press through the nylon of my white
summer cardigan, the elbow folds
into the blanket of her hand.
From elbow to wrist, she holds the long bone,
carries it across the road.

MARY NOONAN

Armour

This body
Is no more than the armour
That an archangel

24

Chose to wear to pass through the world
And, disguised like this,
With its wings wrapped up
Inside of me,
With the visor of its smile
Hermetically sealed on my face,
It goes into the heat of battle,
Is assaulted by injury and insult,
Soiled by vicious looks
And even caressed
On the steel plating of its skin
Beneath which revulsion incubates
An exterminating angel.

ANA BLANDIANA
translated from the Romanian by Paul Scott Derrick & Viorica Patea

If

If my body was a country, it would be
Afghanistan; pregnant with IEDs, problematic, incomprehensible;
If my body was a river it would be
Indonesian Citarum; sluggish, mercury poisoned, cargo of turds
            and plastic;
If my body was an animal it would be
A hyena; toothless, starving, drooling in its concrete lair;
If my body was a colour it would be
That indefinable, infantile impasto of all colours mashed together;
If my body was music it would be
Jangling, angry discords best switched off;
If my body was a woman it would not be
Me.

FRANCES KAY

Nude

(after a portrait by Dominique Renson)

Framed by white wood, a woman stands,
thighs swathed purple, muddied plum,
thick, flexed and worked,

textured to a dense auburn tuft,
resinous between rounded hips.

Square-knuckled fingers
hang limp, curled and shadowy,
familiar in their empty tenderness.

Whereas the stomach's smoothly oiled
pink is smeared in a rich beige tallow,
laboured over, brushed
to where lilac ribs corrugate,
without any mark or mole.

Uneven, light-bulb breasts
illuminate different directions,
capped by nipples daubed peach
soft shading, as if sucked slowly.

And higher, the throat
is ridged by another redbrown thicket,
brushed back from the face
where all movement culminates.

With its dark lips, jutting cheeks,
flared nose and still, clear examination
of the eyes, blue – mine staring back at me.

SARAH HYMAS

I put a pen in my cunt once

I put a pen in my cunt once
just to play with myself
when I was at a loose end
when we were in one of those times
lying in straight lines in the dark
not touching

long milk hands stroke
my words to sour cream
this is what it wrote

DEBORAH ALMA

On New Year's Eve

It's that dangerous lust feeling, that *tonight
why not just let go?* thing and you reach
for the red lipstick, that colour
your mother wouldn't let you
wear as a teenager,
the red of blood dripping
from vampires' teeth,
chilli pepper red hot red,
the kind of red that pouts
and swings its hips;
and there is a frizz in the air
a stirring, a throbbing
dance that enters through your feet and you think
what the hell, and your shoes
match the lipstick, and oh baby
you are so ready,
and when he turns and smiles

all you can think of is cock
and the two of you
in a darkened corner thrusting tongues
and you know
you are going to hate yourself in the morning,
but you have another tequila anyway,
and you slip your hand into his
but only because you like the curve of his arm,
and you may not remember his name in the morning
but right now he's perfect,
and you think what the hell,
you are so ready,
oh yes baby.

KERRY HAMMERTON

He Sees Me

I like this man who
charmed by me
slips alongside and inside of me
like the tongue of a dog
lapping at my life
throwing the ball of it
into the air with joy
to catch me out again and again
and laugh at my earnestness in odd places

he says
he says I rise up like a hundred balloons
let loose from a child's hand
beautiful, bold, even when out of sight
like notes of music falling over themselves
like larks ascending

he says when I sleep I sigh
and he watches me wake and smiles
at the fuzz of my hair and my mind in the morning

he is charmed, he is charmed
I begin to charm even myself
he sees me so lovely

DEBORAH ALMA

Bulimic

Blood dries on the bathroom floor
beside my head as I lie curled in
a foetal ball watching dripping pipes.

I am a dirty puddle of darkness after purging.
In black clothes on a bed of polar tiles
my back yawns bare between a belted waist

and little top, silently awing the still tub.
The dim moon of my body is shocked
by pale shores of arms and neck and face,

made paler still by moonlight and stars.
At midnight the bathroom is hushed.
Ingrained in the circle of my dead gaze

the toilet stops hissing. Innocent
as a lunatic I knelt hours ago before it,
hearing a skinny saint rave within me –

'Empty, empty her and she'll be thin!'
I clung to the covenant like clingfilm
over a rib and heaved her hungers.

Drunk on her breath and bowed
to a cistern I emptied, emptied,
emptied her,

burned her weeds and wiles –
I trespassed into the body's chambers
and raped it with two blistering fingers.

This fire may lick and melt
but it is unforgiving; my fingers
may enter but parch and scorch

in the caustic passion of juices from the gut.
The body weeps, reluctant.
Be wary of it.

She erupts maniacally
until blood makes her holy, barren, empty.
Neither tears nor the easy flush

can patch a ceremony. It escapes
into the eve of thinness.
The cold body keels in honeyed drips

onto tiles; knees collapse,
elbows dance graceless
from the seat; a demented head

falls on a scale, blood trickling from the nose.
Now, curled beside dripping pipes,
weighing the head's load, in black clothes

framing the arms, the neck, the face.
The tiles do not warm the numb.
We move like spirits.

LEANNE O'SULLIVAN

Underneath Our Skirts

Although a temple
to honour one man's voluntary death,
his ceaseless weep of blood,
the women cannot enter
if they bleed –
an old law.

As the bridal couple glides
down the aisle,
her white veil twitching,
I feel my pains.
A woman
bleeding in church,
I pray for time,
for slow motion.
Unprotected, I bleed,
I have no bandage,
my ache finds no relief.
My thorns
are high heels
and itchy stockings.
He, the imitator, bleeds on
in numb eternal effigy,
his lugubrious journey of martyrdom
rewarded with worship.

Tonight custom demands more blood:
sheets must be stained
with the crimson flowers
of a bride's ruptured garden.
Her martyrdom
will be silent knowledge
suffered in solitude.

As we leave the house
of the male bleeder,
I feel myself wet and seeping,

a shameful besmircher of this ceremony
of white linen
and creamy-petalled roses;
yet underneath our skirts
we are all bleeding,
silent and in pain,
we, the original
shedders of ourselves,
leak the guilt of knowledge
of the surfeit
of our embarrassing fertility
and power.

KATIE DONOVAN

Clear Cut

In America, this wilderness
where the axe echoes with a lonely sound
LOUIS SIMPSON

I blame it on our forefathers
who sweated and sawed,

stripped bare the beast until nothing
stood between them

and what they claimed as theirs.
Hills left to scab healed

into cities which raised sons
who satisfied themselves trimming hedges,

pulling weeds, mowing lawns;
sons who found fearsome

the thicket at the slope of our bellies
and decided it was our turn to cut.

KRIS JOHNSON

What Do Women Want?

I want a red dress.
I want it flimsy and cheap,
I want it too tight, I want to wear it
until someone tears it off me.
I want it sleeveless and backless,
this dress, so no one has to guess
what's underneath. I want to walk down
the street past Thrifty's and the hardware store
with all those keys glittering in the window,
past Mr and Mrs Wong selling day-old
donuts in their café, past the Guerra brothers
slinging pigs from the truck and onto the dolly,
hoisting the slick snouts over their shoulders.
I want to walk like I'm the only
woman on earth and I can have my pick.
I want that red dress bad.
I want it to confirm
your worst fears about me,
to show you how little I care about you
or anything except what
I want. When I find it, I'll pull that garment
from its hanger like I'm choosing a body
to carry me into this world, through
the birth-cries and love-cries too,
and I'll wear it like bones, like skin,
it'll be the goddamned
dress they bury me in.

KIM ADDONIZIO

33

The Ugly Daughter

knows loss intimately,
carries whole cities in her belly.

As a child, relatives wouldn't hold her.
She was splintered wood and seawater.
They said she reminded them of the war.

On her fifteenth birthday you taught her
how to tie her hair like rope
and smoke it over burning frankincense.

You made her gargle rosewater
and while she coughed, said
Macaanto girls shouldn't smell
of lonely or empty.

You're her mother.
Why did you not warn her?
Hold her, tell her that men will not love her
if she is covered in continents,
if her teeth are small colonies,
if her stomach is an island,
if her thighs are borders?

What man wants to lie down
and watch the world burn
in his bedroom?

Your daughter's face is a small riot,
her hands are a civil war,
a refugee camp behind each ear,
a body littered with ugly things

but God,
doesn't she wear
the world well.

WARSAN SHIRE

Biosphere

You'll leave the crowded carriage on the train
sucking in all the humanness in your belly
until the dress falls straight down across
your waist, untouched by imperfections.
Your calves built to outrun the unsightly
reflections in shop windows, hair tousled,
catching its breath on your shoulders
because your look has long been
'trying too hard to look like you
haven't tried very hard'.
You are perfumed with
dry, anxious breaths that keep
you only one gasp away breathing in
so much you disappear.

But I wish you would wear yourself like a rainforest.

I want the stubbly bark textures on your legs,
standing end to end,
sweet like cinnamon woodwork.
Your breath humid with songs
you left in your gut because breathing
wasn't fashionable.
The leaves caught in your teeth
like sunlight streaming in.

I'm sure when rainforests breathe,
everything else moves so they can be still.

I want to unravel the guilt pressing your
legs together until you take up the empty spaces
you are too scared to interrupt.
Do not touch your body with bad intentions.
Do not pinch the parts spilling out of
your shirt, or knead the skin
like dough between fingers until it grows
red from rejection. Do not cook it under

the sun because skin was designed to
be loved by warm hands, and not fire.
The hills, road markings, earth and spice
trails on your thriving ecosystem are
sitting under your nailbeds.
They will remind you that
nature has wanted soft mud for your growth,
not steel clippers peeling you back to the root.

Rub your full stomach because you don't have a beard
to twiddle between your fingers.
It is filled with wisdom.

SUNAYANA BHARGAVA

A Clearing

When my eldest son died last week

I ate –

started picking pieces of plasterboard
drilled my tongue into the cavity
wound fibreglass floss round and round.

I ground up breezeblock and brick –
licked every crumb –
chewed tables and chairs,
spat splinters.

In a cascade of foam,
I devoured the sofa –
all its flabby trampolinings,
sick bouts and Sunday snoozes.

I bit the taps off radiators,
gargled at their fountains.
Still thirsty,
I drained and buckled the tank.

Chipping the enamel off the bath gave me a jolt,

Taste of iron returning to my blood,
prickled attraction and repulsion of mild steel
with the pins and plates bracing me, patching me
from times I was knocked down and smashed.

At 5.30, I quaffed the pilot light like a happy hour cocktail,
knew I must go deeper.

On my hands and knees I scratched aside tiles, slabs,
tasted oxides, alloys, amalgams –

I must excavate the gas main,
unleash the blue-hungry flames that snarl from the oven mouth.

CHRIS KINSEY

Pomegranates
(for Lady Macbeth)

I wish that children came
easy as a lie.

That blood came, dropped like
so many seeds –

thoughtlessly. It's as if
someone has sewn me up.

So I took the handle of a knife
and split a slit.

Finally blood, for all the
months I missed.

Imagined: a pomegranate
spilling red-bruised-black

imagined a girl her flesh
was blue and sad

imagined a boy his hair
was black like mine

imagined myself stretched
scream-open and alive.

It took five hours to
stitch me up.

They left my hands red,
so as not to forget.

KIRAN MILLWOOD HARGRAVE

Miscarriage, Midwinter

For weeks we've been promising
snow. You have in mind
thick flakes and a thick white sky;
you are longing to roll up
a snowman, to give him a hat
and a pebbly smile. We have ice
and I've shown you, under

the lid of the rainwater barrel, a single
spine forming, crystals pricked
to the delicate shape of a fir, but
what can I say to these hard
desolate flakes, dusting our path
like an industrial disaster?
It's dark, but I'm trying to scrape
some together, to mould just
the head of the world's smallest
snowman, but it's too cold and
it powders like ash in my hand.

KATE CLANCHY

Churched

My aunties were churched.
Gravelly-voiced women
with low-cut necks
and wide-brimmed hats
and hands that kneaded dough
and slapped it in its place.

'I'll not be churched again,' she said,
me aunty Nora,
sitting there in her frock
of brazen red.

Six children did she bear –
'Sure what's a little wear and tear
for a woman like yourself.'
Two others did she lose,
one was handicapped.
Still is.

'Wombs and breasts and leaking milk, quick
pass us the surplice made of silk' –
That's what she swore
she heard them say,
the clerics
when they began to pray.

'I'll not be churched again,' she said,
'and bow and scrape
and bend my head.'

'Sure what in heaven's name
would they know
of mornings retching o'er the sink,
of the giving up of the booze,
the fags, the drink.
Of the giving up and the giving
In and the hormones
raging through me
like an ocean
full of sin.'

'I'll not be churched again,' she said,
'and bow and scrape
and bend my head.'

'Sure what in heaven's name
could they know
of the life growing
in my womb,
how it moves
and turns, swimming,
in a dark galaxy
of its own,
and how I nightly roam
the barren landscape
of the moon,
then I'm throwing up again
at noon.'

'I'll not be churched again,' she said,
'and bow and scrape
and bend my head.'

'Sure what on earth
could they know
of bringing forth
a child; of the moaning
swelling, growing wild,
of the burning opening
wide and free
and my waters breaking
like the sea.'

'I'll not be churched again,' she said,
me aunty Nora,
sitting there in her frock
of brazen red.

'I'd rather go to an early tomb
than let them curse
my blessed womb.'

SIOBHÁN MAC MAHON

Churching was a religious ceremony, performed by the Catholic Church,
on women, following their giving birth – a sort of cleansing.

The only body I have

I've:

Loved with it.
Told lies with it.
Ate too many mince pies with it.

Dressed it in some questionable clothes over the years.
Poisoned it with drugs.
Filled it balloon like with fears.

Cut it. Bitten it. Watched bits of it sag.
Walked it. Scolded it. Taught it how to nag.

Spent hours looking in the mirror criticising.
Different parts of it every year despising.

Yoga'd it. Toga'd it.
Made it run when it wanted its bed.
Put it through aerobics until every part was red.

Broken little bits of it on several occasions.
Blamed the flabby bits of it for struggling relations.

Called it too short.
Let it be bought.
Sold it down the river.
Taken vodka to extremes without warning my liver.

Dyed its hair. Painted its eyes.
Tried every product possible in efforts to disguise.

Dehydrated it. Berated it.
Burnt it in the sun.
Sat on it. Picked it.
Prayed I'd get a better one.

Tired it. Squashed it.
Failed to de-freckle with lemon bleach.
Scratched it. Starved it,
to be weights always just out of reach.

Bitched about it in its company.
Hated it with all my heart.

But now that it don't work no more
I wish I could go back to the start.

ELOISE WILLIAMS

Chocolate

She crams it down her throat
like a murderess,

alone at last,
alternately *kissing* and *throttling*.

SELIMA HILL

Does My Bum Look Big in This?

Women, beware, for the war is not won;
We're out of our kitchens, no longer Anon,
We run countries and councils, households and firms,
Budgets and hedge funds, all on our own terms.

We broadcast, direct, write, publish, teach
And yet liberation remains out of reach;
For still the enlightened glitterati will hiss
'Can you tell me, does my bum look big in this?'

Celebrity culture is not helping our cause,
With beauty defined by the size of our drawers.
Breasts like bazookas, teeth bleached to fluorescence,
We're expected to stay in endless adolescence.
No wonder our faces look shocked and aghast,
Our looks are what matter and our bottoms are vast.
I'll bet the day of the wedding, Pippa asked her big sis
'Be honest, does my bum look big in this?'

So ladies watch out, if you value your lives,
You're right to be more than just mothers and wives.
If you're fifty and flabby and dress like a slob,
Book in with your surgeon or risk losing your job.
Your degree, your gold medal are not worth a jot
When the circle of shame zooms in on that bot.
When you look in the mirror, remember *Ignorance is bliss*
And don't ask 'Does my bum look big in this?'

PATRICIA ACE

Invitation

1

If my fat
was too much for me
I would have told you
I would have lost a stone
or two

I would have gone jogging
even when it was fogging
I would have weighed in
sitting the bathroom scale
with my tail tucked in

I would have dieted
more care than a diabetic

But as it is
I'm feeling fine
feel no need
to change my lines
when I move I'm target light

Come up and see me sometime

2

Come up and see me sometime
Come up and see me sometime

My breasts are huge exciting
amnions of watermelon
                    your hands can't cup
my thighs are twin seals
                    fat slick pups
there's a purple cherry
below the blues
                    of my black seabelly
there's a mole that gets a ride
each time I shift the heritage
of my behind

Come up and see me sometime

GRACE NICHOLS

Regular Checks Advised

Tits in grubby photographs, the lens puffs them up
like garden birds in winter. Mills&Boon *breasts*,
and the same for the hungry baby in the service station, feeding.
Bosoms for the shop assistant, arms up to let the tape slide round;
something in wire, lace, elastane to hold the *bloody things* down.
They're *mammaries* when suddenly not yours, when
someone with a face like grey water tells you it'll pinch a little,
removes a cylindrical portion of the *puppies* for pornography,
the *bee-stings* squeezed in the playground,
the girls the boys allude to, to be sent to the lab like a dirty text.
Those *funbags* have their interest piqued: you'll hear back in three
      weeks.

ALICE TARBUCK

To a Friend for Her Naked Breasts

Madam I praise you, 'cause you're free
And you do not conceal from me
What hidden in your heart doth lie,
If I can it through your breasts spy.

Some Ladies will not show their breasts
For fear men think they are undressed,
Or by't their hearts they should discover
They do't to tempt some wanton lover.

They are afraid tempters to be,
Because a curse imposed they see
Upon the tempter that was first,
By an all-seeing God that's just.

But though I praise you have a care
Of that all-seeing eye, and fear,
Lest he through your bare breasts see sin
And punish you for what's within.

ELIZA (*fl.* 1652)

Trichotillomania

she plucks out
each eyebrow hair
one by one
with platinum tweezers

and stands them up
on the black lacquer dressing-table:
her row of soldiers
first line of defence

above them, framed
in the oblong mirror:
her deforested forehead
wondering eyes
inconsequential nose
the fleshy lips protected
by a layer of down
(now that would have to go)
her smooth neck
her far too animal body

JANIS FREEGARD

Mobile Gallery of Me.

I am abstract personified.
The graceful 'S' bend
of scoliosis spine.
Swooping slice of lobectomy scars,
picked out in pointillist stitch marks.
Appendix smile knife-stroked
across my belly, gnarl of arthritis
that has turned my hands
to Rackham-style roots.
Cicatrice seams where a new shoulder
and knee were inserted,
marks in flesh like a palette knife's edge.
Worn the way others wear tattoos.
Proudly, extravagantly. Unhidden.
Defiant to the stares, pitying looks.
This is me. Complete with battle scars,
medals, commendations.
Works of art. Bestowed upon me
for surviving.

MIKI BYRNE

Busy Dying

I used to listen to people going on about stuff but
time is precious and I don't any more.
I used to live in Germany
I used to remember the reg. no. of my car
I used to be more organised about paperwork
I used to get paid on Fridays – money in my hand
You rarely see actual notes nowadays.
I used to be in a folk band and sang *Hard Times*

I used to collect bits and pieces in an *Old Curiosity Shop*
biscuit tin. I still have it, full of treasure.
I opened it recently to place a square
of my mother's granny print apron in it.
I used to live in the city
I used to listen to advice from friends
Now I listen to my own gut which is much happier.
My head is too.
I used to be a child. Some days I can still sulk.
I used to believe in *The Waltons, The Little House on the Prairie,*
Flipper and *Tammy.*
I used to look at the news, bought a newspaper every day
but it's all bad stuff.
The beautiful simple, seeing otters at the lake, isn't news.
I used to chew *Wrigleys* gum
I used to know where I left stuff
Now I lose it all the time
Keys, pin numbers, beloved animals, my parents and friends
I'm still losing them.

I used to have two breasts now I have one
I used to think the remaining breast
Should be in the middle of my chest
I felt unbalanced.
It took a year to accept this 'new look'.
I knew I had accepted it when one morning
I was about to shout
'Has anyone seen my prosthesis?'
Wouldn't that be shocking funny?
I rolled back onto the bed and laughed.

I used to be busy dying now I'm busy living.

ROSALEEN GLENNON

A Room of Her Own

For the last sixty years my grandmother
has cut and styled her own hair. It's grown thin,
her scalp shows the colour of communion
wafers, but the shade remains rich auburn.
She stands above the sink secreted in
the laundry-room (where her man will never
seek her out) and coats the strands with stinking
ammonia-scented creams that set while
she sorts the dirty clothes and loads the old
washer. Florida light (constantly spring-
like) pours through the blue glass vases lining
the sill. This is her room, more than bedroom,
where Popie piles his guns; or the lounge, where
she cleans, but never sits. She wouldn't dream
of doing this in their shared bathroom. She
thinks of this as her time. Her sole selfish
pleasure: making herself beautiful for
him. The washer chugs and sloshes, spreading
soap suds. She rinses the dye down the drain,
a dark, stinking spiral, drags a wide-toothed
pink comb (hers since the 50s) through darkened
curls, selects her scissors and starts snipping.

BETHANY W. POPE

Bowled, again

Please cut my hair so that I look like
me, but with shorter hair – and can you do this
without me trying to describe what it is
that I expect to see when I next dry my hair –

50

for the polite gene in me knots grimly in curls
to your scissors and even if it's scrimshaw
on a grand scale and even if I go home
and wash my hair ten times to get rid
of the belted Galloway in the mirror,
I will still leave you a generous tip.

And what's more, come back
in a month or so as if I am a goldfish.

KRISTINA CLOSE

And then he said: *When did your arms get so big?*

Oh honeybunch, they're not *big*,
they're fat – and every wibbly inch
a rich memory card. This quarter turn
under the left arm, this alabaster,
is the Boston pie last summer,
strident and merciless

and this by my elbow
is the most perfect jam doughnut
I ever had, its sugar curtain
parting, the command performance
stroking my tongue,
its belly dancer middle
jewelled and shadow dancing
with my teeth.

But this here, this favour under my arm
was the perfect cream eclair –
oh my dear, the parting of the slice
and pastry, a thousand naked
wind blown men running bobbly

through the lawns of the National Trust
in Surrey, the ladies in the kitchen
pressing, pressing, into the dough.

KRISTINA CLOSE

High school

Better than the fractions like weird pictograms,
better than *Othello*'s major themes, the queens
and kings of Scotland down the years,
titration, verbs in conjugation tables
you can still recite – the sound let out
before the thought's complete – *Je suis.*
Tu est. Il est. Elle est. What you learned best
was the fact of your disgustingness.

How vile you were. Your every flaw:
the monstrous, speckled thighs that brimmed
from gym shorts, ringed with red elastic welts
and howled down in the changing rooms.
The shoes: too flat, too high
you slattern, too gum-soled and scuffed,
or not enough. The hairstyle that your Mum
still cut; your Mum; the blush of rage

or shame that spread routinely up
your neck. Your ugly neck. Your neck,
never adorned with friendship beads or, later,
hickies. Your score of same; of love-notes
passed to you in class, slow-dances, gropings,
fucks – all zero – kept with everyone's for broadcast
in the midst of something good, the way
a dying rock-star breaks the evening news.

It's women who learn first the throw that hurts,
the way to really wound your fellow girl,
the soft parts where it doesn't show
and cannot heal. How did these blue-eyed whippets
learn so much of power and spite in years
you'd spent just grooming dolls and waiting,
fanning gravel out behind your bike's
bald, beaded, tinkling wheels?

The worst thing: they believed it all,
the tiny hierarchies built and smashed
at rum-and-cola parties you were never party to.
They thought that life would always hold
the door for them, or for their looks, their smart
high-kicks – did it matter which? – and you'd always be
some chubby joke. You believed it too.
The softest part of you believes it now.

CLAIRE ASKEW

Utility Room

The air was thick,
it reminded me of my utility room
on cold December mornings
where my mother stood in the doorway
a trembling cigarette in one hand
and a tear stained tissue in the other.
He stared at his computer screen
blatantly avoiding eye contact,
he made jokes
but he did not laugh,
and tried to smile
but found he couldn't,
he asked me if I ever harm myself;

what an open question,
we all harm ourselves in one way or another,
we all drag our bedsheets around the house
dank with the smell of expectation,
filled with our uncertainties
and our dark
haunting desires;
to not be alone,
to not be alone any more,
'do you?' he persisted,
I gave a little laugh,
'I suppose I do.'

PHOEBE WINSTANLEY

Marks

Shadiya just slides her sleeve up
'I wanted to tell you about these.'
And Nawal wears her shirts short
Her dancer's arms marked in red grid lines
Today covered and crossed over
With luminous green graffiti.
And me, me I come home and bite my thumb
Bite my palm
Bite my wrist
Tooth marks like a sweet candy bracelet
The imprint of incisors
My alligator skull.
It breaks my heart that they're only twelve
But I mock myself, at almost thirty,
For still being here.
What, then, is the optimum age
To cut, to break?

I sit on panels where professionals discuss copycat behaviour,
A rash of disclosures from Year Eight.
And I started after Amelia started, it's true,
After she slipped a craft knife from her hand luggage and begged
      me to hide it.
After I went to look for her, wondering if she'd made it to her
      dreaded nightshift
And found on top of silk throws and Swedish language magazines,
A gorgeous wooden box, a deluxe set, artist's blades.

When the children come to me, each worrying about the other
In their Noah's Ark pairs, Shakespearean twins
I say as they care for their friend they must care for themselves too.
I read psychiatry journals, see those words – lacerate, mutilate,
      auto-aggression.
Under 'copycat' these reasons are proposed:
Awareness – that this is now on their 'menu of options',
Attention-seeking, and a desire to belong.

I do not want this panel of professionals to know.
Our list of pupils under 'serious concern' – this is not a group to
      which I
Wish to belong.
I have no mastery over intolerable feelings.
I am harming my sense of myself.

LEAH WATT

Good Friday

It was the day I chopped off my own head
and blundered around the kitchen.
No eyes to see myself with
I felt strangely at peace.

The kitchen became an obstacle course
but I touched heat and hollow,
put my head in a pot to boil
to still my breath and hush my tongue,

and when I was tender and quiet
I served my head up on white china:
apple-mouthed and gristle-chinned,
heard your delighted gasp.

JULIA WEBB

The Woman Who Talked to Her Teeth

She'd had her teeth out in her teens.
Lots of girls did it.
Dentists were expensive:
you got fitted with a false set
before marriage and kids.

What did she want with teeth?
She'd still got a jagged scar
where the neighbour's dog
had bitten her cheek.
She didn't even make bridesmaid.

She kept her lips shut
to hide the hole in her mouth.
She ate the kind of food
that slipped past her gums:
gallons of soup and ice cream.

They talked her into it for her Sixtieth.
False teeth were different now:
pearly, better than real.
She could have a perm, too.
And a new party dress.

She agreed, wanting the dress.
But the teeth never went into her mouth.
She'd lay them on the grass,
jaws slightly open
so they seemed to be smiling.

Then she'd sit beside them
(at a safe distance,
in case they turned nasty)
and tell them the stories
she would have told her children.

VICKI FEAVER

Friendship

I lay naked on the medical table
his hand pressed up against my sternum,
searching for the rhythmic thump of my heart.
I feel no shame, no compunction.
He sees my breasts in all their youthful glory,
is touching them foreign from a lover.
Chest bruised and turning to purple,
he tells me to hold my breath.
Whistling in the darkened room
letting out a low, 'Wow'.
If we were making love, this would be climax.
I look at the screen and watch the smooth walls of my heart pulse,
He smiles at me and croons,
'Has anyone ever told you
that you have a beautiful mitral valve?
I bet you get that all the time.'
'Ya know – you're the first.'

Laughing, I stare at the ceiling
savouring the compliment –
at least my heart is beautiful.
Hand to heart, I laugh and laugh.

CAITLIN BAGLEY

Flesh

Sitting in a doorway,
in October sunlight,
eating
peppers, onions, tomatoes,
stale bread sodden with olive oil –

and the air high and clean,
and the red taste of tomatoes,
and the sharp bite of onions,
and the pepper's scarlet crunch –

the body
coming awake again,
thinking,
maybe there's more to life than sickness,
than the body's craving for oblivion,
than the hunger of the spirit to be gone –

and maybe the body belongs in the world,
maybe it knows a thing or two,
maybe it's even possible
it may once more remember

sweetness,
absence of pain.

KERRY HARDIE

This Woman

The moon pulls at me like a tide.
On these winter nights, my bones feel brittle
and my knees are sore from praying.

By day I leave the cats with their backs to the fire.
I try to forget about my body that feels like a house.
The house I grew up in because it's always so cold.

I dream of eels and believe I can feel a pair
of warm hands around my girth but they evaporate when I wake.

The locals lay branches of mountain ash on my doorstep.
A Wicklow man instructs me to urinate outside
for the blood to flow, cover every blade of grass, he says.
My mother made me drink a pint of buttermilk
and as she does, I wonder if my salt-skin will ever feel quickening.

NICOLA DALY

Embarrassed

I thought it was okay, I could understand the reasons.
They said, 'There might be a man or a nervous child seeing
this small piece of flesh that they weren't quite expecting.'
So I whispered and tiptoed with nervous discretion.
But after six months of her life sat sitting on lids,
sipping on milk, nostrils sniffing on piss
trying not to bang her head on toilet roll dispensers
I wonder whether these public loo feeds offend her
because I'm getting tired of discretion and being polite
as my baby's first sips are drowned drenched in shite
I spent the first feeding months of her beautiful life
feeling nervous and awkward and wanting everything right.

Surrounded by family till I stepped out the house
it took me eight weeks to get the confidence to go into town.
Now the comments around me cut like a knife
as I rush into toilet cubicles feeling nothing like nice.
Because I'm giving her milk that's not in a bottle
wishing the cocaine generation white powder would topple
I see pyramid sales pitches across our green globe
and female breasts – banned – unless they're out just for show.
And the more I go out, the more I can't stand it
I walk into town, feel I'm surrounded by bandits,
because in this country of billboards, covered in tits
and family newsagent magazines full of it
W.H. Smith top shelves out for men
Why don't you complain about them then?
In this country of billboards, covered in tits
and family newsagent magazines full of it
W.H. Smith top shelves out for men
I'm getting embarrassed in case
a small flash of flesh might offend.
And I'm not trying to parade it
I don't want to make a show
but when I'm told I'd be better just staying at home
and when another friend I know is thrown off a bus
and another mother told to get out of a pub
even my grandma said that maybe I was sexing it up.
And I'm sure the milk-makers love all this fuss
all the cussing, and worry, and looks of disgust
as another mother turns from nipples to powder
ashamed or embarrassed by the comments around her
and as I hold her head up and pull my cardie across
and she sips on that liquor made from everyone's God
I think, For God's Sake, Jesus drank it
So did Siddhartha, Muhammad, and Moses
and both of their fathers
Ganesh, and Shiva and Brigit and Buddha
and I'm sure they weren't doing it sniffing on piss
as their mothers sat embarrassed on cold toilet lids
in a country of billboards covered in tits
in a country of low-cut tops, cleavage and skin
in a country of cloth bags and recycling bins

and as I desperately try to take all of this in
I hold her head up, I can't get my head round the anger
towards us and not to the sound of lorries
off-loading formula milk
into countries where water runs dripping in filth,
in towns where breasts are oases of life
now dried up in two-for-one offers, enticed by labels
and logos and gold standard rights
claiming breast milk is healthier powdered and white,
packaged and branded and sold at a price,
so that nothing is free in this money-fuelled life
which is fine if you need it or prefer to use bottles
where water is clean and bacteria boiled
but in towns where they drown in pollution and sewage
bottled kids die and they knew that they'd do it,
in towns where pennies are savoured like sweets
we're now paying for one thing that's always been free,
in towns empty of hospital beds, babies die,
diarrhoea-fuelled, that breastmilk would end.
So no more will I sit on these cold toilet lids
no matter how embarrassed I feel as she sips
because in this country of billboards, covered in tits
I think we should try to get used to this.

HOLLIE McNISH

For Lucy

If you are a woman, you are allowed
to write about wombs, your relationship
with your mother, your lover leaving, your
lover leaving with your mother, wombless,
and the way you feel about your wombless
mother-loving bastard child. Period.

61

You may do so in lyric utterance
only. Moon images crowd the work like
a lunar eclipse, and if you can get
Aphrodite in or post-Freudian
metaphor, they'll call your power female.
But what if you're rubbish at ironing
analogies. What if your speakers want
to, well, speak instead of singing. Voices
loud and raucous and – face it, babe – more
like the birds you find in prose. Ah, that makes
them prosaic. Women fucking, cursing
their way through blank verse, scrunching handfuls of
post-partum skin and plugging holes that won't
shrink back to size. Coating their lungs cosy
with fags, drinking neat scotch of a Wednesday,
eating crusty fig rolls with tuna straight
from the tin and spilling the oil on their
best work top. We'd best not write about them.

So we'll diet off this too-too flesh, and
moon over growing things and baby's smiles.
Try to remember to hate our mothers
or to claim sisterhood with their bloody
wiles. We'll stick our fingers in our ears in
case the odd fuck or you're having a laugh
gets through. Commune with fertile soil (even
though, quite frankly, these hands are raw and clapped
with scrubbing them one hundred times a day),
and milk our tits – no, teats, I'm sorry – for
what they might be trying to say. Curdled
body-words. Not able to look in a
mirror. Not able to look. Bloated with
body-shame; anorectically eaten
for breakfast. Ironically rhyming moon
with June. Not able to look. Not able.

If you leave off one s, wombless becomes
Wombles.

CARON FREEBORN

Room 204 (Double for Single Use)

This is the room of tongues,
their busy pink-on-pink textures:
rose plush, plum chintz, the tiles
in the bathroom as marbled
as their meat when spiced and tinned.

Look at the placement of mirrors:
the wall-sized gilt affair alongside
the pilastered bed, swallows
the room in its gold-lipped mouth
and returns it redder and less itself.

Most of all it is not from the bed
but beside the bed, that you note
someone has angled an oval glass
on the mahogany chest of drawers
so you see your pear-shape precisely

from the back as you climb
onto the high mattress. An unordinary
thing: that candid peach-satin-framed
rear view. Intimate for single use,
you claim this tanless, tapered skin.

All the kittens' rough tongues
are talking at once under the black beams
like a ship creaking its timbers
as you dip and swim in the watery
fetch between mirror and mirror.

JUDY BROWN

Pair Bond

The talk in the bar lulls a half-time fill:
as I knife-scrape the head from another pint,
he hovers, pocket-foothering his change.

Steadying for the ask, he addresses
my full frontals, my baby buggy bumpers,
my Brad Pitts, my boulders, my billabongs,

my squashy cushions, my soft-focus bristols,
my motherly bosoms, my matronly bulk,
my Mickey and Minnie, my Monica

Lewinskys, my Isaac Newtons,
my snow tyres, my speed bumps, my Tweedle twins,
my milk makers, my Mobutus, my num-nums,

my Pia Zadoras, my Pointer Sisters,
my honkers, my hooters, my hubcaps, my hummers,
my Eartha Kitts, my Eisenhowers,

my God's milk bottles, my Picasso cubes,
my chesticles, my cha-chas, my coconuts,
my dairy pillows, my devil's dumplings,

my objectified orbs, my über-boobs,
my one-parts Lara, my two-parts globe,
my skyward pips, my lift and separate,

my airbags, my feeders, my mammy glands,
my Bob and Ray, my big bouncing Buddhas,
my sweater stretchers, my sweet potatoes,

my rosaceous rotors, my trusty rivets,
my melliferous melons, my mau-maus,
my tarty, my taut, my pert palookas,

my jahoobies, my kicking kawangas,
my agravic gobstoppers, my immodest maids,
my Scooby snacks, my squished-in shlobes,

my cupcakes, my soda bread, my bloomin' baps,
my brilliant bangers, my brash bazookas,
my windscreen wipers, my Winnebagos,

my wopbopaloubop bopbapaloos,
my yahoos, my yazoos and yipping yin-yangs,
my paps, my pips, my pommes-de-terres,

my pushed-up, plunged-down, paraded balcony,
my slow reveal, my instant appeal,
my décolletage, my fool's mirage,

and I watch him pay up, steady up and leave.

BARBARA SMITH

The Beast Is Dead, Long Live the Beast

It was the difference between us that got me at first
it was vast, unambiguous. He held me as if I were glass,
saw mere delicacy as I sharpened my blade for the feast,
eyeing his girth like a wife at the butchers. 'All of you,'
I thought, 'I want all of you.' He watched with a soft look.

I preferred the smashed crystal, the roars, or nights
I heard whelps, spied blood on his loose gums, remorse
on his muzzle. He presumed I was sweet, a double-centred
chocolate treat, longing for my own breed, not something
entirely different. Then, oh hell, he told me.
True love's vow will break this curse.

I took a scented soak, pondered his request. Recalled
how I saddled his back, toured the estate, my knuckles
white on matted fur, my womb tumbling, tumbling...

He sighed and paced, till the third morning, on which
he collapsed as if shot, his light almost out. It's now or never.
I had a smoke, considered... his eyes would remain the same
and those howls, they came from within. 'Truly,' I said, just
in the nick, 'I love this beast and promise to be his.'

Fur smouldered to reveal fine skin, smooth limbs, a face
as pretty as my own. I couldn't watch. It was grotesque. I left
the prince to admire his pale fingers, a pleased tilt to his lips.

In the woods, I got lost. Galloped for hours, for days
devoured small creatures, tossed sour entrails to the fox.
Circled. Didn't rest. Beast, where was my beast?
How I missed his stride, his tattered fur, his terrible voice.
I swore to die before sacrificing life to that, that pretty boy.
In the end, he trapped me.

Mister Ruby Rings, Pointed Slippers fetched a posse
twelve hounds, and a net. Looked at me as if we never
sweat in the dark, tore the moon, swallowed stars...

I masquerade till my escape. It's easier by day.
When I dream I wake with blood on my dress.
The house frowns. Stone Venus is contemptuous
the bitch. He awaits an answer to his latest request.
Marriage. 'Bite me baby,' I hiss.

NIAMH BOYCE

For Her, a Different Skin

Given the right blade, he might knife her.
Not for fox pelt sleekness, or rabbit warmth.

Hang legs from a rafter, limbs parted.
Not for the lush flush of raw pain.

Unseam a red circle; cut deeper.
Not for a bitter scream's squeezed juice.

Slice the underside, finger it from bone.
For the guts' intricacies, untangled.

Slide away cartilage, loose from flesh.
For the pulsed butterflies, released.

Free intergluing membrane, slowly unsplice.
For the cracked almond heart, relieved.

Glide hand between, peel from carcass.
In hope of finding skin which fits,

without snicking any arteries.

SARAH JAMES

Refined to bone

Mirror mirror on the wall
I want my body curves
refined to bone.
A little more discipline
more fruit, less fat
will make me all
I ever wanted.

Six stone and losing.
Still too fleshy, slack.
Protruding organs spoil the line
like bra straps, ugly
through a cotton top.
Five stone, ten.
At certain angles I can like myself
but turn this way and still
I see the pulse corrupt the skin,
the swollen shape of womb.
My monthlies stopped three pounds ago.
Five stone, three.
These doctors cannot keep me
from my target. Nearly there.
Only you I trust, my
mirror mirror on the wall.
You'll see me pure
refined to bone.

JEAN GILL

Unmade

My art is not refined –
pleasing to the eye like
                           the still-life
gape of a Vermeer maid. I don't
coax paint into golden sunrises.

Tracey has big tits and comes
(on her own terms)
from Margate.

My body blinks neon
in a cycle of open
                       and closed
signs through cracked glass.

Spontaneity can never be
considered a genuine mode
of artistry. Emin uses pop culture
                                        strategy –
a certain native cunning.

My bed is the last punch
on a Margate street
after a 3 a.m. lock-in –
blood spilling over the frame
of my B-list set.

Emin's a woman artist
who fucks –
                    a lot.

My sheets are the damp heat from my body
after sex, the wet wreck-
age, how it freezes
into week-old stains –
yellow and gathering dust-
mites, like moths, to feed on flames.

Bad-sex aesthetics
                        and radical
permutations of feminist art.

My underwear is stained
red – not by menstrual blood –
but by globs of stigmata.

Emin puts her pain on
to attain fame and notoriety.

My tent is covered with names
of friends, lovers, kin...
and drunkenly, even the man

who opened me when I was thirteen –

                            taught me

not to let the wound heal,
but to pick the scab until it bleeds.

ELISABETH SENNITT CLOUGH

Nuptial Song

I got married
I got married to myself
I said yes
a yes that took years to arrive
years of unspeakable suffering
of crying with the rain
of shutting myself in my room
because I – the great love of my existence –
did not call myself
did not write to myself
did not visit myself
and at times
when I'd get the courage to call myself
to say 'hello, am I well?'
I wouldn't come to the phone

I even put myself
on a list of pains-in-the-neck
I didn't want to talk with
because they drove me nuts
because they wouldn't let me alone
because they backed me into corners
because I couldn't stand them

at the end I didn't even pretend
when I asked if I was there

I let myself know
tactfully
that I was fed up with myself

70

and one day I stopped calling myself
and stopped calling myself

and so much time
went by that I missed me
so I said
how long has it been since I called?
ages
it must be ages
and I called myself and I answered
and I couldn't believe it
because though it's hard to believe
I hadn't healed
I'd only been bleeding
then I said 'hello, is that me?'
It's me, I said, and added:
It's been a long time since we've heard
I from myself or myself from me

would I like to come over?

yes, I said

and we met again
in peace

and I felt good with myself
and myself as well
felt good with me
and so
day after day
I married and I married
and I am together
and not even Death can me part

SUSANA THÉNON
translated from the Spanish by Maria Negroni & Anne Twitty

Rock 'n' Roll Mamma

They've skinned up, chilled, unpacked their sleeping bags
and dirty shirts. They've used up all the mugs
and scoffed our hard-earned bread, they've blocked the stairs
with piles of giant shoes. The dizzy air's
well hammered. This is rock 'n' roll: guitars
propped against walls like casual strangers, vast
monoliths of amps, hard riffs and licks,
the slick of sweat and beer, the scent of sex.

I wonder if they'll let me in to watch the dawn.
Am I condemned to be some Mrs Robinson,
but fatter, hiding in my pantry
with my garters and my cupcakes? Me?
I knew it once; I still know it; the crash
and roar. Mud, rhythm, skin; no lull, no hush.

I'll try for ecstasy. I'll build the fire.
You think I'll give in to crimplene, retire
to bridge and camomile? No fucking chance.
My acid days are done, but watch me dance.

JACQUELINE SAPHRA

Wolves

She had lived with the wolves till she was three, they said:
to her, time was measured only by the period she was with the wolves
and what came after.

To them the wolves were unfathomable beasts
because they paid homage to the moon with their song
and tore at flesh with their precise teeth.

But to her it was them – the men who stared
at the flowering teenage girls with the hunt in their eyes,
their cold lengths of metal – it was they who were the beasts.

So she narrowed her eyes when they spoke to her
and once, when the odiferous one touched her throat,
she turned and made a hole in his cheek with her precise teeth.

And she was glad that because she had lived with the wolves,
because she spoke few words and because of her precise teeth,
the men never stared at her like that.

BECKY CHERRIMAN

Madame's Menu

For an appetiser, we have the Luscious Lucia.
She recently turned 21 and is a lean size 6.
With slender legs, our Latino Lovely has olive skin,
a sun-blushed 34D bust and lime-green eyes.
A High-class Escort and Exotic Dancer,
she's a flexible filly who'll slip around the stiff pole
to give you one-on-one exclusive performance.

Or perhaps you'll settle for Lucy.
She's 25 and a skeletal size 6.
She's a barmaid and single mother.
She lives with a dealer who is
clever with his fists.
Gang-raped on a girls holiday in Ibiza,
she now uses narcotics and sun-beds
to bleach the pain.
Her gums bleed, her face: leathery.
Her favourite snort is cocaine
but she'll settle for amphetamine.

Our main dishes this evening include:
Top-Choice Tori who is 24 and a perfect size 8.
With honeyed hair and baby-blue eyes,
she's a High-class Escort and Glamour Model.
She has succulent breasts and curves
in *all* the right places with a busty 32C cup.
She is bronzed all over.
She's a spicy, saucy, sexy lady
who loves to tease and aims to please.

Or, there is a second choice of Toni.
She's getting on a bit at 32, and is a size 10.
With peroxide extensions, blue contact lenses,
she's a cam-girl and cervical cancer survivor.
In a *Wonderbra* and tutu she models for favours.
Abused by her stepdad then evicted at 14,
she turned tricks to survive.
But, with a convincing wig and a painful smile
she'll give the infamous Tori tit-wank
and say it was just for you.

For dessert we have the Naughty Nikita.
She's only 18 and is a slim size 6.
With a tiny waist and a pert bust,
our Russian Princess has
hot-chocolate hair, full cherry lips
and sweet almond eyes.
She's a student nurse and
a high-class escort.
She's a girl-next-door type.,
who'll give you a one-on-one
full girlfriend experience.

Or perhaps you would rather a Natia.
She's 19 and a pre-pubescent size 4.
Originally from Prague,
she worked the stag scene.
Arriving in Britain just one month ago
she finally escaped the grip of her pimp.
She has frizzy hair, sallow skin
and a Meth Amphetamine problem.

Living alone in a bed-sit hole,
she can't speak English.
But for a little extra she'll swallow,
and moan convincingly as you drop
your load in her mouth.

Finally, for wine, we recommend Wines Ruby
who is one of our more mature ladies, at 29.
She's a curvaceous size 12 and a buxom 34G cup.
Deliciously voluptuous, she's a High-class Escort
and Plus-size Model.
Full-bodied with fruity notes,
auburn hair and silver eyes,
this lady has ripened beautifully with age.
With class, wit and style,
she's the perfect accompaniment
to any occasion.

Or perhaps a bottle of Rita.
At 42, she's a mother of 5 girls.
Due to a diet of cider and processed food
she's diabetic and overweight.
A part-time cleaner and dinner-lady,
she has greying hair, flaky dermatitis
and scarred wrists 'from the fryers'.
Her fella is on Disability Benefits,
he calls her a fat slag
and drinks twelve cans a day.
She's been on the game
for over a decade
and can't give up
because it puts food on the table.

GEMMA HOWELL

Dowry

A car, a house and ten lakhs.
Initial outlay for a virgin deal.
My share in a co-operative,
invested to the maximum
in a nest and egg –
a hopeful future.

I have paid into this scheme
pledging a mortgaged body
on a high yield fund.
Fingers crossed, counting
on multiplying his shares
increasing his stock
promptly.

My deeds lie locked
in his banker's vault.
And he has the power to foreclose.
The tally-keeper, abacus leader,
tracking my course in a monthly audit.
Flowing into the red
is not an option for him,
or for me.

For he can abuse a profitless bond
in kerosene, liquidate a capital loss,
and released, speculate again
on another's portfolio.
While I am staked and branded
worthless, in a graveyard market.

SHASH TREVETT

The Green

D'aller là-bas vivre ensemble!
Aimer à loisir,
Aimer et mourir
Au pays qui te ressemble!

CHARLES BAUDELAIRE

I'm bleeding out on the Green
and there are ass bandits standing by waiting for someone better
with a hole less unpredictable, less full of teeth and silent screams.
I am bleeding out on the Green waiting
for a whole human being to emerge. But it's too soon.
Maybe I am that human. Maybe you are half of it.
Maybe there's nothing even
about what we might make.
Maybe I'm making human being
seem too important.

Workers are tossing gold geraniums into a barrel
pulling them whole from the ground
and I keep seeing the same guy
wearing a dog collar everywhere I go. He has mud
on his velvet boots and he looks me in the eye
as if to say the mud is old mangoes and the mud is old
hearts and the mud is old books that I gave away or let rot.

There is space and there
is space
I tell you.

And there is disgrace.

In Germany they scrub out
their trashcans.

Old nature didn't ask for this.
To be the receptacle of our fantasies. Old nature didn't say
pick me to be the woman

77

turned into a map and charted and uncharted
for the sake of what you think you don't know.
Her *mons pubis* is the treasureland and her breasts the entryway.
A good thing cartographers knew something about foreplay.

I am bleeding out on the Green
and the Green could be anywhere
suffused with whatever meaning I say.
Like the Green is Florida's sea grape trees
with roots that trip me up as horseshoe crabs
flee my heavy *Fleurs du mal* step
and old women toss grapes into a bowl to make
sea grape jelly to scrape onto crackers for schoolchildren
to make them see the land is important, to keep them from building
more high-rises and boating over more manatees
and refusing to turn out their lights that make turtle
hatchlings march toward Wal-Mart
instead of the sea.

Or the Green is St Stephen's in Dublin
where cops with long capes once shielded
men pissing straight liquor onto the grass
but never the women with blood on their thighs.
The best I could do is enter a pub
where the snug's walls have been taken down
now that women can be trusted to mingle
in the whole space and order their drinks at the bar
instead of through a little window with a sliding door.
But the snug is in my mind as they say.
A painful dialectic. The snug
is where you cut yourself down to half. Where you say no
to half, where you can say anything at all, and it's
of no consequence. There is space and there is
space I say. A useful dialectic. The snug is where you go
to talk about bleeding out on the Green. The snug is where you go
and keep yourself on guard. The snug is only in my mind. It's
            not real.
Right. I can do anything, go anywhere
and no one will touch me. Least of all when I am bleeding
out on the Green. Least of all when I am the old woman

picking sea grapes. Least of all when I am helping nature refuse.
When I am taking this blood right out.
When I am taking out a whole human. Being. Or a half. My half.

Or the Green is generality. As though that's possible.
The *Generalife* gardens of the Alhambra
where the flowing water is louder
than my mind where the snug is still built
louder than the ping of sea grapes
in the metal bowl. Step onto the Green.
Bleed out. Breathe out. In.

KIMBERLY CAMPANELLO

Anuva Bun inee Ovun

A'rite? Nairmz Rhiannon,
an I leve on thuh Rock.
I luv drinken ciduh,
an I luv sucken cock.

I wanna bee yin college,
buh I go' uh lickle kid.
An-uh crèche in college
aint tha fucken big.

My muvva wun elp me,
cuz I nict er tellee.
An my ole man iza preck.
Ee puncht er in th'bellee.

Nutz in skool, I wuz.
Chucken chairz un sellen fagz.
Expelled ut firteen, I wuz,
f'robbin uh teachuz bagz.

79

It wuz f'thuh best ough,
I wuz pregnunt wiv Levi,
Mist all uv my examz, I ded.
Tuh my life I sed g'bye.

My felluz shaggen round,
iss bin gor en ona wi-yul.
Iss bairbeez bout t'drop soon.
Weyull gor on Jeremee ki-yul.

Sor, I angah round uh shops,
tuh see oo eez shaggen.
All-uh boyz cum on tuh me,
finken *I'm* out slaggen!

My boobs uh fucken killin
An my belleez rock ard.
Bastad duzunt giva shit,
now eez wiv iz new tart.

Anuva kid.
Anuva Giro.
Iz tha all wee-yuh werff?
Iz ent air more too wis yere life
un givin fuckin berff?

Anuva drink.
Anuva fag.
Anuva spliff,
or pill.

Wee-yuh fucken ewmuns yuh,
not pigs in fucken swill!

GEMMA HOWELL

Rock: Slang term for Graig-Y-Rhacca council estate, in Rhymney Valley,
South Wales. English translation: Rock of Dawn.

Rape Joke

The rape joke is that you were nineteen years old.

The rape joke is that he was your boyfriend.

The rape joke it wore a goatee. A goatee.

Imagine the rape joke looking in the mirror, perfectly reflecting back itself, and grooming itself to look more like a rape joke. 'Ahhhh,' it thinks. 'Yes. A *goatee*.'

No offense.

The rape joke is that he was seven years older. The rape joke is that you had known him for years, since you were too young to be interesting to him. You liked that use of the word *interesting*, as if you were a piece of knowledge that someone could be desperate to acquire, to assimilate, and to spit back out in different form through his goateed mouth.

Then suddenly you were older, but not very old at all.

The rape joke is that you had been drinking wine coolers. Wine coolers! Who drinks wine coolers? People who get raped, according to the rape joke.

The rape joke is he was a bouncer, and kept people out for a living.

Not you!

The rape joke is that he carried a knife, and would show it to you, and would turn it over and over in his hands as if it were a book.

He wasn't threatening you, you understood. He just really liked his knife.

The rape joke is he once almost murdered a dude by throwing him through a plate-glass window. The next day he told you and he was trembling, which you took as evidence of his sensitivity.

How can a piece of knowledge be stupid? But of course you were so stupid.

The rape joke is that sometimes he would tell you you were going on a date and then take you over to his best friend Peewee's house and make you watch wrestling while they all got high.

The rape joke is that his best friend was named Peewee.

OK, the rape joke is that he worshiped The Rock.

Like the dude was completely in love with The Rock. He thought it was so great what he could do with his eyebrow.

The rape joke is he called wrestling 'a soap opera for men'. Men love drama too, he assured you.

The rape joke is that his bookshelf was just a row of paperbacks about serial killers. You mistook this for an interest in history, and laboring under this misapprehension you once gave him a copy of Günter Grass's *My Century*, which he never even tried to read.

It gets funnier.

The rape joke is that he kept a diary. I wonder if he wrote about the rape in it.

The rape joke is that you read it once, and he talked about another girl. He called her Miss Geography, and said 'he didn't have those urges when he looked at her anymore', not since he met you. Close call, Miss Geography!

The rape joke is that he was your father's high-school student – your father taught World Religion. You helped him clean out his classroom at the end of the year, and he let you take home the most beat-up textbooks.

The rape joke is that he knew you when you were twelve years old. He once helped your family move two states over, and you drove from Cincinnati to St Louis with him, all by yourselves, and he was kind to you, and you talked the whole way. He had chaw in his mouth the entire time, and you told him he was disgusting and he laughed, and spat the juice through his goatee into a Mountain Dew bottle.

The rape joke is that *come on*, you should have seen it coming. This rape joke is practically writing itself.

The rape joke is that you were facedown. The rape joke is you were wearing a pretty green necklace that your sister had made for you. Later you cut that necklace up. The mattress felt a specific way, and your mouth felt a specific way open against it, as if you were speaking, but you know you were not. As if your mouth were open ten years into the future, reciting a poem called Rape Joke.

The rape joke is that time is different, becomes more horrible and more habitable, and accommodates your need to go deeper into it.

Just like the body, which more than a concrete form is a capacity.

You know the body of time is *elastic*, can take almost anything you give it, and heals quickly.

The rape joke is that of course there was blood, which in human beings is so close to the surface.

The rape joke is you went home like nothing happened, and laughed about it the next day and the day after that, and when you told people you laughed, and that was the rape joke.

It was a year before you told your parents, because he was like a son to them. The rape joke is that when you told your father, he made the sign of the cross over you and said, 'I absolve you of your sins, in the name of the Father, and of the Son, and of the Holy Spirit,' which even in its total wrongheadedness, was so completely sweet.

The rape joke is that you were crazy for the next five years, and had to move cities, and had to move states, and whole days went down into the sinkhole of thinking about why it happened. Like you went to look at your backyard and suddenly it wasn't there, and you were looking down into the center of the earth, which played the same red event perpetually.

The rape joke is that after a while you weren't crazy anymore, but close call, Miss Geography.

The rape joke is that for the next five years all you did was write, and never about yourself, about anything else, about apples on the tree, about islands, dead poets and the worms that aerated them, and there was no warm body in what you wrote, it was elsewhere.

The rape joke is that this is finally artless. The rape joke is that you do not write artlessly.

The rape joke is if you write a poem called Rape Joke, you're asking for it to become the only thing people remember about you.

The rape joke is that you asked why he did it. The rape joke is he said he didn't know, like what else would a rape joke say? The rape joke said YOU were the one who was drunk, and the rape joke said you remembered it wrong, which made you laugh out loud for one long split-open second. The wine coolers weren't Bartles & Jaymes, but it would be funnier for the rape joke if they were. It was some pussy flavor, like Passionate Mango or Destroyed Strawberry, which you drank down without question and trustingly in the heart of Cincinnati Ohio.

Can rape jokes be funny at all, is the question.

Can any part of the rape joke be funny. The part where it ends—haha, just kidding! Though you did dream of killing the rape joke for years, spilling all of its blood out, and telling it that way.

The rape joke cries out for the right to be told.

The rape joke is that this is just how it happened.

The rape joke is that the next day he gave you *Pet Sounds*. No really. *Pet Sounds*. He said he was sorry and then he gave you *Pet Sounds*. Come on, that's a little bit funny.

Admit it.

PATRICIA LOCKWOOD

The Shave

That night, he nailed her plaits to the floor,
split the dull cotton of her skirt and vest
to shave from her the coppery threads.
The hair wound around his lithe left hand:
his right held a blade – snip-snap at the best
of her golden head and off it came on the bedsheets.

The severed hair spelled a ladder
with rungs that could carry a man.
Smeared and shucked like an oyster,
bald and grey like gristle, jellied and numb
as masticated food, she had nothing
to keep from him and nowhere to hide.

ZOË BRIGLEY

Trunk of fig tree from Ses Rossells

This tree is a grey-faced woman
who struggles to her feet, one arm
a broken branch hanging useless
The wild fire on the hill
you have escaped for now
but you are tinder-dry this summer
Terracing lies tumbled around you

Earlier we stood in the gloom of the cave
wondering why we had come
Inside, the usual debris
human excrement, tissues, rusting tins
a goat's skeleton picked clean by ants
blackened stones of a makeshift hearth
To please our father, find his fabled cave
we had scrambled over boulders

cut ourselves on razor-grass
and now your arm is broken
Two daughters in their fifties
still trying to prove
they are as good as the sons he wanted

We should have followed the example of Vassilissa
borne the goat skull home
and let the darkness in its sockets
blaze our rage, burn down the house

ANNA CROWE

Where It Hurts

Let me tell you what like it is.
It's a great muckle hand inside my guts, clawing.
Or a camshachle crow; beak at my kidneys.
See the way yon thing over there is moving?
Well, it moves like that. Like a verb.
There's the thump, the weight falling – *here*.
Give me your hand; that's it,
across my chest. Heavy, like the battle o' Culloden.
Oh Christ yes. Don't kid yourself; I'm not kidding.
The body is a bloody battlefield.

These knees of mine are full of fluid.
See, feel. Don't be gentle. *Push*, prod.
God, you can almost hear the sea in my knees;
there's so much water, slapping, slopping,
slobbering at the shore. I'm away the trip.
You could cross the water; you could speed bonny boat
and still not reach me – bird on a wing.
My illnesses just keep coming; going out-in, in-out.
I've been sick since time immemorial.
Since the days of the plague, the black death;

since the rain of the frogs, cats and dogs.
I could throw myself up and never come back.
Chuck myself into the sea, the North Sea.
The black water would gulp me down, whole.
I don't think I'd so much as wave,
I'm that sickened with myself. Sick.
Sick. Sick. Sick to death of being sick.
Always spoiling everybody's fun.
Lying down when people are up and about.
In a dark room, when people are laughing in light.

I go to the Doctor but what does the Doctor say?
He looks at me as if I were a germ, a sudden outbreak.
When did you start feeling this way? he mumbles,
already scribbling my sentence, my fate.
What's the disease inheritance? What's in the family?
What odd traits have been passed down? Background?
Christ! I come from a long line of sufferers.
We lived with live-in disease-ridden beasts.
We caught rabies, had babies, passed madness down.
We clenched our crossed teeth.

Sick to the back Scotch teeth.
I could spit my teeth out on stone floor –
too many scones, treacle scones, fruit scones,
currant loaf, malt loaf. Crumble. Too much sponge,
light sponge, heavy sponge. Dumpling. Shortbread –
too many rhubarb tarts, custard creams, eclairs.
My blood sugar is soaring. My tongue is so sugary
I flatter my enemies. My healthy, blooming enemies.
I say sweet things when I want to weep and spit.
They tell me I'm looking well; lies – I'm peelie-wally!

Today people tell the sick they look well.
A leper never had to suffer compliments.
If I could say I had consumption, spotted fever,
cholera, smallpox, tuberculosis, apoplexy, let's say,
any classic would do: hookworm, bookworm, bubonic plague.
If my house had to be fumigated, smoked with sulphur;
if I could suffer a rosie on my face, eggs in my groin;
somebody might take me seriously, might listen.

If I could have a day, an ordinary day,
away from the worry – the body – I would be happy.

How can I be happy when loss is greeting round the corner?
Let my body fill with poison, bacteria, culture
while the workers go to the pictures or opera;
culture with a choc ice, tub of vanilla.
Let my body swirl with my hosts,
let the wee life-forms dance and flounce,
shaking their big bellies; sobbing, multiplying.
Madame Butterfly, Tosca, Treponema.
You clever bastard, bacteria, always a new story.
Oh bacteria, bacteria; *wild*, the sea moans.

Up to here. I've had it. *Here.* C'Mere.
I'm a guillotine at my own neck. Chop.
My neck is as stiff as a donkey's cock.
I can only turn round this far – look.
It's got that bad I've started to swear.
I've begun to think in obscenities, I can't stop – cunt.
How did I get like this? So far away from myself.
I used to love ballads, folksongs.
I will go I will go when the fighting is over.
But the fighting of the body is never over.

The stars are white cells. There is no beauty.
When you are sick like me,
day in day out, sunrise, sundown, it spreads.
Like the illness spreads. Across fields, memories.
My eyes see right through the body to the bad bits.
The scary bits cowering inside the flesh.
Growths that people don't yet know about.
I can see it coming. It's not just me.
The tinge of green, the yellow eyes, the shaky
hands, the puffy face, the tell-tale signs.

True, true. Some are braver than me: I'm not
brave. I've gone from one time to another
puking, spewing; bloated, swollen.
Sick as a parrot, a gambler, a joke, a dog, a mind.
Sick as a simile, sick (sic), a poet, a plant.
Drooping, limp, languid, flaccid, fatigued.

Bored to death, belching, burping, breaking wind.
Oh the terrible ennui, the listlessness of illness.
Oh the repetitive answers: 'How are you?' 'Not so good.
Could be better. Seen better days, Don't ask.'

You can't say I haven't tried everything.
Hypnotherapy, acupuncture, homeopathy, reflexology.
My tarots read. My chart done. See that astrology!
Psycho analytical psycho therapy. Alexander's Technique.
Moved my three-piece suite. Rubbed seaweed on my feet.
Something meant to unblock my energy. Synergy?
Brown rice and bananas for breakfast, dinner, tea.
Nat Mur? Wasn't that my remedy? The sea in me.
My homeopathic personality: I hoard painful memories;
I nurse grievances; I don't forgive; I take offence easily.

Don't say I haven't tried to be well. I've tried.
I've smiled. But what's a smile but an attempt to hide tears.
Many's the time, I've gone out unwell, near collapsing.
A burning pain straight down the middle of the throat.
Dead centre. Like somebody's lit a line of gunpowder.
The sick headache tightening the screws. Zigzags.
My moods swing. My sinuses scream. I look like a hag.
There's not a pain I haven't had.
I could paint the pains on a big white sheet.
The weary wabbit world of the worried unwell.

It's not just me is it? I'm not the only one.
Were we always this ill? Was I?
When we die is the sensation heavy, light?
I'll die a weighty, hefty, heaving death.
Other light people around me might take flight
like graceful swallows. But I'll be a huge pig
squealing. A fucking great buffalo roaring.
What a big bitter pill to swallow
– will it be red, will it be yellow?
After all I've been through. A great thumping death.

A fucking great fucking big death.

JACKIE KAY

Question

Body my house
my horse my hound
what will I do
when you are fallen

Where will I sleep
How will I ride
What will I hunt

Where can I go
without my mount
all eager and quick
How will I know
in thicket ahead
is danger or treasure
when Body my good
bright dog is dead

How will it be
to lie in the sky
without roof or door
and wind for an eye

With cloud for shift
how will I hide?

MAY SWENSON

Infertility

Doctors have their ways to investigate: microscope eyes
that count the glittering fish of sperm, cameras that stalk
beaded eyes into the gorgeous-red heart of the cervix.
The ultrasound wand probes, presses, sucks to measure the orb
of each egg in its sac, while x-rays unravel the womb,
a stretched concertina that spasms even as it fills
with saline. Later there's chemical mingling of your blood
and mine, to map how XY arms and legs of chromosomes
embrace or fist. Here I am in the stark, unforgiving
sonographer's light: a passage, narrow key, squat cave
gorged by blood, or just a ripening plum with arid seeds.
Here am I, a woman not a body, in the snowlight
outside the hospital, where I smear the whitened sidewalk
and run with my long legs, my pretty body still unveined,
still to be spoiled by the loving-soft fat of motherhood.
So many women come to me saying, 'I have lost too,
and this one, and this one.' So many embryos retreat
to flesh: the live cell of the mother. Don't tell me that it
will happen for me, when the only sure thing is a miracle:
the sperm nuzzling in its nest and the egg that opens, explodes.

ZOË BRIGLEY

Bog Child

(after 'Punishment' by Seamus Heaney)

She left footprints that I sink into neatly.
They tell me of her idle dreams
as she drifted through this place of peat
and dark pools, a stillness interrupted

by hooves crashing in the thick growth
when a man on a white horse
took her up before him
and galloped her away from birdsong warning

of treacherous ground underfoot.
Patient, the bog waited
in the knowledge that he'd shuck her
from the horse as easily

as the farmer tosses sacks
of fuel into a tractor's turf-box – the same
she rode on as a baby
grinning and jammy-fingered –

that she'd soon lie loose-limbed in the grass
insistent sunlight prying at her closed-eye shells
bogland hungry for her bones.
The slow digestion.

As the poet disturbed the young temptress
from her long sleep in the bog
now let me draw myself in your mind
to emerge from a seam of memory

when you've all but forgotten.
My fingers are twisted to roots
my darkened face etched with the musings
of peat. My heart

is a clutch of birds – watch them
cascade upwards to scraps
of cloud like bog-cotton, fleeing your step
your notions of excavation.

RÓISÍN KELLY

Meditation

*There's a brown girl in the ring, fa lala la la la
There's a brown girl in the ring fa la la lala lalala...*

Let me do a meditation on skin.
Skin.

Let me do a meditation on tongues
Tongues clicking Xhosa, tongue nailed to a gatepost.

Let me do a meditation on eyes.
Eyes calabash brown drowning in the blue from a Dutchman.

Let me do a meditation on hands
Hands smooth over bottom whipped by licks, plantation
kisses, Brixton boys hungry for Caribbean ass.

Let me do a meditation on ears
Ears seduced by Kyrie Eleisons, rock-steady, Jimmy Cliff
Dylan Thomas, djembe beats,
A lover whispering 'just a little finger in your panties sweetness'.

Let me do a meditation on noses
Noses pulled straight into European beauty
Assailed by patchouli circa 1971 in a Kingston
(upon Thames) dancehall, Led Zep and Yes and ganja shared
In a purple bedsit, Richmond, Surrey.

Let me do a meditation on legs
Show me your motion Baby
Arms limbo limbering up limbo baby
Breasts the bounty and burden babies of.

And that woman undulating down a city street
Walking like she has the world at her feet
Rolling like a ship braced to withstand every goddam wave
Know this and weep, let me do a meditation on feet
Watch the universe opens as she barefoot passes.

MAGGIE HARRIS

Country cousin

My cousin Mabel writes four times a year.
We've never met, but our mothers were so close,
when they traded bonnets they were mistaken one for the other.

Mabel fills her letters with devotion to the styles
of the changing seasons: her new wine-coloured silk
(the periwinkle has been turned for second-best),
flounces bound with black velvet, ruffles and puffs and gloves,
fichus of lace. She always asks, with copperplate regret:
but my country cousin, so far from shops and fashions,
what will you wear this season?

I wear God's own territory, these western plains that he made flat
so he could watch you run and run for days, and never lose sight
        of you.
I wear my feet bare and frilled with dirt, the way Indians do,
and wish my eyes as black and keen as theirs.
I strain the seams of my calico dress when I shock wheat with the
        boys;
instead of flirtations, I offer healthy arms and breath.
With my ungloved hands I weave rags into rugs to adorn my floors
        for the new season,
and I open Mabel's next letter. She'll gush about the new styles in
        bonnets,
making me a gift of her wine-coloured silk
because it's been supplanted by the new season's shade –
dresses shining with the humble colour of wheat.

TRACEY S. ROSENBERG

The Liberator

When our feet hurt, we hurt all over
SOCRATES

When Grettie from Grealish Town
soaked and clipped –
you talked.
You'd tell her things
you kept from the priest.

At first there were doubts
about this whippersnapper
who worked in the hat factory.
What would she know
about stubborn old nails?

But the toenail gang knew her unflappable touch.
She would tuck cotton wool soaked in antiseptic
under an untameable bucko and deliver him.

You'd feel nothing more than her coaxing gaze
calling for, more story, more story.

RITA ANN HIGGINS

Leaving My Hands Behind

I have decided that they are partisan
or at least, not to be trusted.
For all the things they've touched, helped, held
there are a thousand they've broken.

They're happy to be let go. Perhaps I'll see them
out and about, wearing sovereign rings,
nails painted with miniature Chinese dragons.
Maybe I'll get a wave, or the finger.

I'll begin a new life
where a blink can shut me off,
where I will never touch, only be touched
and I'll pull my horns in like a snail.

JESSICA TRAYNOR

Cunts and Cocks and Balls

I'm allowed to stay the night with my friend when I get to be
        fifteen.
We spend the afternoon trying on her five pairs of Levis.
That night we eat avocado and sit round a wooden table
all wearing Levis; me, my friend, her little sister and
her big sister, her mum and her dad. No one says anything
about the Levis, just about how there isn't enough avocado to go
        round.
I save my wages from working in the greengrocer's each Saturday,
hauling steaming beetroot out of a vat and sorting potatoes
and hiding from the Saturday boy who makes me feel
red as a beetroot; then I buy a pair of Levis. My mother finds them
where I've hidden them. In our house no one wears jeans
because they are worldly. I'd been changing into them
behind the neighbour's garage and going to my Saturday job
where the Saturday boy sometimes touches my bottom and says
        it's nice
and I wonder how it will feel when he kisses me and what I
        should do.
My mother has tears in her eyes and says she must tell my father,
and when she does he takes my jeans and pushes them into the Aga,
where he'd burnt *The Prime of Miss Jean Brodie* the week before.
(At eighteen I leave home, and later, when my mother can bear to
        speak to me again
I bring my boyfriend home and she buys him a pair of Farah
        trousers to wear because

96

she says people can see his cock and balls through his Levis, only
        she doesn't actually say
'cock and balls' but I know that's what she means.)

I'm at a family party and I'm wearing my Levis. My niece is
        getting married
and we're all here to meet the boy. He flirts with me and I
enjoy it though I'm surprised because I'm fifty and he's half my age.
I look at the outline of his cock and balls beneath his jeans
through my sunglasses. We all drink and he gets flirty
with everyone and we all love him till he starts telling jokes.
He tells us about a girl whose camel's foot is so fat it makes
him queasy. And about how he'd like to give my niece a string of
        pearls.
Later I ask my husband, what is a camel's foot? He says
it's when a lady's cunt is big, you know, when you can see it.
Like when she's wearing a tight pair of jeans. If it sticks out.
I feel a sort of sorrow inside me, about my niece, and
about my cunt as well.

SALLY ST CLAIR

Animal (1975)

In that sunny squat, while Stevie Wonder
talks his book on the turntable, she sits
on the sofa found in a skip, holding

a mirror in her hand. The glass circle
shows an animal there. Her stare meets
a lazy, crooked eye, half-closed

in a defiant wink. Her cheeks pink.
But on the bus to work she lets her knees
fall apart, gives leg-room to the creature

she saw framed in shafts of light:
a salty, rough-coat, brindled beast
without a friendly name to call her own.

CAROLINE GILFILLAN

Breaking Fish Necks

The next afternoon we tried anal sex
and as you coaxed my neck with your thumbs

I thought of Wolf's Creek
and the fish you wouldn't catch,

plump trout necks you couldn't bear to break
and take home dead to your mother.

In the warmth I knew my arse
was soft, the downy peach.

But what was beyond drew you in:
a core, sensitive, harsh

like a peachstone –
its coarse ridges, fine strings

caught in grooves
where flesh is torn raggedly away.

Here, at the kernel
of spine, cat's-cradle of muscle,

you tried to undo me, cupping my hips
with your hands, breaking me patiently.

As we paused, I did loosen
but held together

around this hardness,
in the brace of your arms

till we rolled apart
and I healed slowly over.

You stopped fishing years ago.
You only used the stillness,

the bronze film of water
to will the fish deeper.

You couldn't watch them
choke on air or feel the snap

of delicate bones
between forefinger and thumb.

Or walk the mile home
swigging a beer

with a wet chill on your hands,
and flashes of silver skin

too easily become
the dead weight of flesh

slung at the bottom
of your pack.

SALLY READ

Rutting

There was nothing simple about it
even then –

an eleven-year-old's hunger
for the wet perfection

of the Alhambra, the musky torsos
of football stars, ancient Egypt and Jacques Cousteau's

lurching empires of the sea, bazaars
in Mughal India, the sacred plunge

into a Cadbury's Five Star bar, Kanchenjanga, kisses bluer
than the Adriatic, honeystain of sunlight

on temple wall, a moon-lathered Parthenon, draught
of northern air in Scottish castles. The child god craving

to pop a universe
into one's mouth.

It's back again,
the lust
that is the deepest
I have known,

celebrated by paperback romances
in station bookstalls, by poets in the dungeons
of Toledo, by bards crooning foreverness
and gut-thump on FM radio
in Bombay traffic jams –

an undoing,
an unmaking,
raw
raw –

a monsoonal ferocity
of need.

ARUNDHATHI SUBRAMANIAM

In Praise of Footbinding

Women are undergoing surgery to create perfect genitalia
BBC NEWS

The night is soft and dark as plums:

how beautiful the blossom in moonlight,
pale as rice grains.

How beautiful the vulvas of young girls
asleep in their narrow rooms.

In the morning there will be marriage-talk.
In the morning the cutting will begin.

This cut is called Opening Lotus Bud –
it will please the husband.

This, Undiscovered Pearl – choose it
also to stir pleasure.

And this. Silken Pavilion, and this, Perfect Peony,
will please greatly,

all the lovers will be delighted
with the sculpted vulvas of their brides

who until this moment had not known how much
the unsteady feet of their great-grandmothers

– tiny, tiny – excited their husbands,
how the husbands were so delighted

that they wept.

LESLEY SAUNDERS

Honour killing

At last I'm taking off this coat,
   this black coat of a country
   that I swore for years was mine,
   that I wore more out of habit
   than design.
   Born wearing it,
   I believed I had no choice.

I'm taking off this veil,
   this black veil of a faith
   that made me faithless
   to myself,
   that tied my mouth,
   gave my god a devil's face,
   and muffled my own voice.

I'm taking off these silks,
   these lacy things
   that feed dictator dreams,
   the mangalsutra and the rings
   rattling in a tin cup of needs
   that beggared me.

I'm taking off this skin,
   and then the face, the flesh,
   the womb.

Let's see
   what I am in here
   when I squeeze past
   the easy cage of bone.

Let's see
   what I am out here,
   making, crafting,
   plotting
   at my new geography.

IMTIAZ DHARKER

The Dowry

Look at my daughters,
count them if you wish.
Look at their shoulders
taut and cool as grape skin.
The lovely way they sit,
in control of the Plaza;
there is power in stillness.
Look inside their heads,
do you like it in there?
What do you see? You must
be mistaken – look again.
Look at their brooches
set with jewels from the mid-afternoon:
the fly, the ant, the last drop
of dew from the Alderman's lips.
Look at the gold strung teeth
smiling across their throats.
Have you finished counting?
Well, count them again.

JANET ROGERSON

Five Years of Growth

My mother is aghast. It's taken five years to grow it,
and I've no answer she'll accept because I just don't know

whether it was the heat – 105 Fahrenheit in the shade –
or the weight of it that oppressed me, or whether

it was the sound of next-door's lawn mower grooming
the unruly August grass, or even the rock and roll

of next-door's boy, whom I fancied, who didn't fancy me,
his quiffed head turned forever towards my spotty friend Vicky,

and though he taught me to fish one afternoon; evenings
I could see them miming sex with their clothes on

through her kitchen window; or whether it was university only
a week away, but eight hundred desert miles away

in another state, that made me gather my ponytail, my long,
beautiful ponytail, into a tight rubber band, that led me

to the sewing scissors that were dull and grumbled all the way down
to the stubble, chewing through five years of growth,

or whether it was the unbearable idea of freedom. Snipping to shape,
the dyed-red hairdresser diagnosed *typical seventeen*,

but I must have guessed that freedom was whistling towards me
like the San Joaquin daylight whizzing towards L.A.

WENDY KLEIN

Darling Kisses

When we snogged, I was Mum's
trendy yoga friend Trish. You were Kev,
Trish's imagined fella. It was after *Dynasty*
when we kissed and 'did it'
by shaking our clothed bodies together
like Torvill and Dean in the *Bolero*.
'Darling Kisses' was our name for this –
you had to whisper 'ooh darling!' first.
We weren't close. We were on top of each other.

The massages began at Gran's house
with Mum-style tickling of the neck. Next came
animals traced down spines and my hand, just shy
of your forest – it was all teeth
and Disney wolves. I think of the forest
in Cardross with the ruined high-rise seminary
that in my childhood was a closed order. Today
its rooflessness is crowned by birds. Its altar
is an altar to needles and fallen angels and weather.

ANNA WOODFORD

White Asparagus

Who speaks of the strong currents
streaming through the legs, the breasts
of a pregnant woman
in her fourth month?

She's young, this is her first time,
she's slim and the nausea has gone.
Her belly's just starting to get rounder
her breasts itch all day,

and she's surprised that what she wants
is *him*
    inside her again.
Oh come like a horse, she wants to say,
move like a dog, a wolf,
           become a suckling lion-cub –

Come here, and here, and here –
but swim fast and don't stop.

Who speaks of the green coconut uterus
the muscles sliding, a deeper undertow
and the green coconut milk that seals
her well, yet flows so she is wet
from his softest touch?

Who understands the logic
behind this desire?
Who speaks of the rushing tide
                    that awakens
her slowly increasing blood – ?
And the hunger
              raw obsessions beginning
with the shape of asparagus:
sun-deprived white and purple-shadow-veined,
she buys three kilos
of the fat ones, thicker than anyone's fingers,
she strokes the silky heads,
some are so jauntily capped...
              even the smell pulls her in –

SUJATA BHATT

genderality

1978

aged thirteen / i wear a denim waistcoat /
khaki small-collared shirt
knotted with a black silk tie /
my mum refuses to leave the house /
with me until i take the tie off /
i stuff it in my pocket and wear /
an imaginary knot; centre-stage

scene one:
throw me a life
buoy sailor, we living
in sink or swim times;
all mouth and no trousers
getting thrown out the ladies
for looking so sexy butch
she's a girl!
she's a boi with a toy
denied admission to Vanilla
she's a girl
looking straight / through me

she's all fired up on T
did i say she?
i mean he, it,
shit, we're crossing over, under / cover
agents for the gender divide
becoming them and finding:
recipes for bombs
measurements for inside leg
how to grow the hair / elsewhere
he's a faery boi / should be a girl,
grew his hair and tucked his cock down
her inside leg
what a drag, not popular like the queens / not cultured
like the queers, something in-between the word-play
translator or impersonator
transgressor or impresser
test the line

scene two:
skirts don't suit me, something about the cut,
the print, the way it hangs like abandoned washing
grazing my knees, bellowing in the breeze
an embarrassment / like the time I walked down
market street with the back of it all tucked up in my knickers
and I never knew / that I could wear genes
charity-shop retro, inherited from the underground
worn lives / gender uniforms on rails /

try them on for size / unwanted garments / on special offer /
shop-soiled
y change what you wear / to fit in with your x's crowd
you still won't gain entry / they'll be wearing top man /
when you're all tammy girl

scene three:
on the street I wear one of my off-stage identities

and an old lady says: 'can you help me cross the road young man'
i readjust my sock / take my hands outta my pockets,
grasp her arm, dodge the 6pm traffic

scene four:
i can rip-saw / use a lathe, make mortice, tenon and dovetail joints
'tie your hair back' the journeyman says / health and safety
i plane oak, wafer thin curls peeling back to smooth contours, trace
the years with my index finger /
28 and still no sign of an identity; carpenter, film-maker, web-
           designer
activist, mentor, chairperson
gendered jobs / apply within

scene five:
write an application / person specification:
silver wisdom in her hair
roses / spirals / Celtic knots
big / bouncy / / bra-less / breasts /
stunt cunt flying open
four armed lesbian kali gender killer
this flavour is not available in other stores

MAYA CHOWDHRY

Vintage

Saturday's dress was someone else's, boned
so that it might have stood up on its own.
I wished I could have known its previous owner;
not just a London wife who had outgrown
the kind of life that needs a scarlet dress,
but a starlet, rubbing ice cubes on her breasts
to keep them pert. She'd sleep cocooned in corsets,
she'd be the broad who walked into his office
that drink-fogged Monday, something on her mind,
fur-lapped, with trembling lips, or a barefoot bride
skipping town, thumbing trucks down on neon strips.

Praying, I tugged the zip and slipped inside
another woman's skin, as if her sweat
had stiffened the seams like a salt-rimmed glass.
Oh, I was tits and hourglass hips and ass,
a viciously nipped waist, its hold as delicious
as a lover's embrace.

Of course, it kept its shape
later, when I stepped out of it. The rude
shock of nipples and dark cloud of hair
(no underwear) – I walked, like treading water
warily to bed, my skin's pale lustre
somehow more flawed, nude as a shucked oyster.

SOPHIA BLACKWELL

A Fallow Blooming

She gasps awake from dreams
of wildfires and deserts
to find the sheet scorched in her shape.
Hazy with heat, she staggers
towards a cool shower, closes dry eyes
and sighs as water spits and sizzles off her skin.

Drinking through pores she stands
through days and nights.
Steam clouds into mist, billows from
the window, spirals to suck in air
heavy with spore and seed.

Still, she drips and steams as lichen
grows on eyelids. Tendrils of creamy roots
twist between her toes and cluster under
sagging breasts. Creepers drape shoulders,
caress down her legs, insinuate
over floor and under doors.

New leaves unfurl, shine
with moisture; drip on buds
that swell, bloom and burst
to pollinate the laden air.
Hummingbirds blur to weave nests
from hair, jewel-bright frogs nestle
on mossy thighs and next-door's errant macaw
preens on her shoulder, indifferent to posters
on telegraph poles and trees.

ANGELA FRANCE

Antidote to the Fear of Death

Sometimes as an antidote
To fear of death,
I eat the stars.

Those nights, lying on my back,
I suck them from the quenching dark
Till they are all, all inside me,
Pepper hot and sharp.

Sometimes, instead, I stir myself
Into a universe still young,
Still warm as blood:

No outer space, just space,
The light of all the not yet stars
Drifting like a bright mist,
And all of us, and everything
Already there
But unconstrained by form.

And sometimes it's enough
To lie down here on earth
Beside our long ancestral bones:

To walk across the cobble fields
Of our discarded skulls,
Each like a treasure, like a chrysalis,
Thinking: whatever left these husks
Flew off on bright wings.

REBECCA ELSON

Peach Season
(for Bob)

If the dirt of my body came
straight from the Okanagan Valley
the fat of them would taste of peaches.

Nipples, taut and high as baby birds
stretching out for food, choke
on the excitement of new life and you
touching me for the first time:

the bees of your fingers and thumbs
buzz little circles into my flesh, find something
that feels like a marble rolling under the skin
and I remember

the mammogram, how it turned them both
to fruit leather – flattened, so that the breastedness of them
spread out until they were nothing – and I remember
how it felt. I remember.

I break the silence to tell you
they're fine, I'm fine
but the sting of intimacy
leaves a mark on everything it touches:
I know you know what cancer feels like.

The best peach I ever had came all the way
from British Columbia: a yolkful of fruitedness,
a line creasing down the skin of it,
making cleavage – it was the closest thing
to having something holy in my mouth
and I swear it glowed going down my throat.
It was March when you sent that text
to tell me *I miss your boobs*, and even though
peach season was long gone

I went to Penney's, found a t-shirt with two shells
on the front – one for right there and there, where
the nest of my breasts rests, where the sting
of intimacy left its mark – and I thought

I'll wear it the next time, help you find them again:

two birds cupped in your hands
bring back the taste of peach to your mouth.

DIMITRA XIDOUS

Picnic

It's a cone biopsy. Or a picnic in the sky.
The women lie around with their legs in the air
and the doctor and nurses drift in on clouds.
The women lie back and lie back – they
hadn't realised how far back they could go.
But still the scalpel hops towards them.

Hops and flies of its own accord,
quicker, knowing exactly where it's going.
The women float away from the paper cloth
the clean white picnic plates. The scalpel
has a tiny beak to peck at the women
who hide at the back of the sky

where the weather comes from.
The uncertain weather.

MONIZA ALVI

Falling down, falling down

If I ate no cake,
if I ate two cakes,
if I lingered by biscuits,
disdained cauliflower,
if I had not turned
my face to the sun
if the man had not rushed
from the petrol station
dodging before me,
like you, a dancer,
if I had glanced down –

Is that my blood?
Are those my glasses?
That tooth will cost –
Thank you. Oh no!
Not an ambulance.
And don't call my husband.
I am used to this.
I have fallen off horses.
New raw, rich blood
drops warmly through tissue.
I will call A & E,
I promise. I lie.

'You've done it this time,'
says the bathroom mirror.
My lip is two rags.
With the stained flannel clasped,
I set the cool yogurt,
the crisp and cruel celery
safe on their shelves.
Then I call upstairs.

If I shut my eyes
in Gloucestershire Royal
at one a.m.

I can tick them off,
the London trip,
the din of the party,
falling, falling. Here instead
is a girl, in a wheelchair,
slightly less battered
than my changed face.
Her escort swears,
black-eyed, black-coated,
at stern Reception:
'They want me sectioned.'
They may be right.

Falling, falling
at Gloucestershire Royal
a fair-faced girl
pulls the threads tight,
white skin, rose flesh,
like plaits on a pony,
my black blood clotted,
thick as the night.
'How many stitches?'
'Ten,' she shimmers.
Put back the cake.
Walk out, upright.

ALISON BRACKENBURY

The Room of Coughing

Sometimes you think someone's next to you, coughing aloud
so that you spin round, reaching to touch them – too late.
Yet the coughs are like the murmurs of a restless crowd

as though you were in a dormitory or hospital at night,
where inmates dream on narrow beds, twisting, sighing.
If you strain to hear, after a while you can tell the coughs apart,

know which belong to newly-borns, which to people dying
as though you'd seen their colours, milky, yellow, rust;
each cough carries something else, a bird's shriek, someone saying

do widzenia, a grain of pepper, coil of smoke, the dust
of a city's rubble. How did you ever think all coughs were the same
when each one catches on a different note, some gruff with thirst

others wet like salt spray. Rancid perfume – Givenchy, Guerlain –
fibres of wool or glass, mould on wallpaper, clinging like tar
or spores of fungus and leaf along every string of phlegm;

in each black bubble, mixed with feathers, gristle, fur
and sticking to every drop of mucus, every childhood blood spot,
pine resin, petrol – you feel it all then gasping for air

you hear your own cough rattling in your throat and inside it
your mother's – a bitter taste, cigarettes she finally gave up,
alcohol fumes, scent of roses, a heavy snow cloud and inside that

her mother's raucous wheezing, a floor creaking, something trapped,
footsteps in passages, a tickle of down, scraping of a knife,
more smoke between the gaps, buckets clanking, the water's slop;

cut of a whip across her face, kick of a child against the lining, ice
breaking, horses' screams, refrains which bring you back
to that first splutter in the dark, the forced exhalation of a life
and always like a forest fire her crackling asthmatic hack.

MARIA JASTRZĘBSKA

Dress

You would not have worn it in the kitchen
where the air was stifling, where between
times you sat for hours at the big table
poised in a wrap-around apron. I never
saw you in it working the kitchen garden.
It was not the place, your legs dusted
in dried dirt, where you tended runner beans,
raspberries, young greens and potatoes.
Nor would you have worn it on the high street
where you gossiped in a knotted head-scarf,
a plain basket threaded on one arm.

It was on special days, family days, holidays
in high summer you filled it with flesh.
A creamy fabric dashed with maroon
and lemon flowers swished as you turned, laughing.
Colours you loved. An abundance of buds.

MARY MATUSZ

Poem at Sixty
(for myself)

Now I am sixty
an upstart planet:

my reeling centre of gravity
wrung from its axis,
has steeled itself,
squared the circle
of rearrangements;
freshly-ruched with non-familiars,
wrangling shapes;

117

sharps, flats
and untoned naturals,
key changements?

Ageing pictures
held to the light
make me smile;
there's nothing in these old nostalgias,
landslides, appliquéd words in black and white;
here and here, an interval,
a few remembered notes become accordant
shades of former wrongs
            and right:

Ricking joints and ligaments just about get along,
they snag and snip, gone for a song;
I am a new map, a stand-up routine;
less hip, more fool than cool,
and hair, my dear, must surely, now,
be for the chop? I have been
most carefully
advised to get a crop,
so, from now on,
mine, of course,
will always,
always be
too long:

Even so, I like me now
I like this rimpling belly,
these puckish, softly-sly unseasonals
shaken rightlywrong:

My newly-spannered hands
broach their crinks and corrugates;
I study this late-wrought mileage with esteem,
fastidious veins, disciplines,
process of an evident kind?

It is as if Mozart and Schubert
won't replace Dylan and Aretha,

but simply steepen abroad what these deft
nerves and senses have altered, deepened
and left behind.

VICKY SCRIVENER

Recognition

Things get away from one.
I've let myself go, I know.
Children? I've had three
and don't even know them.

I strain to remember a time
when my body felt lighter.
Years. My face is swollen
with regrets. I put powder on,

but it flakes off. I love him,
through habit, but the proof
has evaporated. He gets upset.
I tried to do all the essentials

on one trip. Foolish, yes,
but I was weepy all morning.
Quiche. A blond boy swung me up
in his arms and promised the earth.

You see, this came back to me
as I stood on the scales.
I wept. Shallots. In the window,
creamy ladies held a pose

which left me clogged and old.
The waste. I'd forgotten my purse,
fumbled; the shopgirl gaped at me,
compassionless. Claret. I blushed.

Cheese. Kleenex. *It did happen.*
I lay in my slip on wet grass,
laughing. Years. I had to rush out,
blind in a hot flush, and bumped

into an anxious, dowdy matron
who touched the cold mirror
and stared at me. Stared
and said I'm sorry sorry sorry.

CAROL ANN DUFFY

Self-Portrait, Rear View

At first I almost do not believe it, in the hotel
triple mirror, that that is my body, in
back, below the waist, and above
the legs – the thing that doesn't stop moving
when I stop moving.
And it doesn't even look like just one thing,
or even one big, double thing
– even the word saddlebags has
a smooth calfskin feel to it,
compared to this compendium
of net string bags shaking their booty of
cellulite fruits and nuts. Some lumps
look like bonbons translated intact
from chocolate box to buttocks, the curl on top
showing, slightly, through my skin. Once I see what I can
do with this, I do it, high-stepping
to make the rapids of my bottom rush
in ripples like a world wonder. Slowly,
I believe what I am seeing, a 54-year-old
rear end, once a tight end,
high and mighty, almost a chicken butt, now

120

exhausted, as if tragic. But this is not
an invasion, my cul-de-sac is not being
used to hatch alien cells, bald peens,
gyroscopes, sacks of marbles. It's my hoard
of treasure, my good luck, not to be
dead, yet, though when I flutter
the wings of my ass again, and see,
in a clutch of eggs, each egg
on its own, as if shell-less, shudder, I wonder
if anyone has ever died
looking in a mirror, of horror. I think I will not
even catch a cold from it,
I will go to school to it, to Butt
Boot Camp, to the video store, where I saw,
in the window, my hero, my workout jelly
role model, my apotheosis: *Killer Buns.*

SHARON OLDS

Stella and Flavia

Stella and Flavia, ev'ry hour,
   Unnumbered hearts surprise:
In Stella's soul lies all her pow'r,
   And Flavia's, in her eyes.

More boundless Flavia's conquests are,
   And Stella's more confined:
All can discern a face that's fair,
   But few a lovely mind.

Stella, like Britain's Monarch, reigns
   O'er cultivated lands;
Like Eastern tyrants, Flavia deigns
   To rule o'er barren sands.

Then boast, fair Flavia, boast your face,
    Your beauty's only store:
Your charms will ev'ry day decrease,
    Each day gives Stella more.

MARY BARBER (*c.* 1690-1757)

Longbarrow

Beauty's on the inside, so they say, but they don't know –
who can judge my clutch of soft and pulsing organs that
pump – flux-stop-reflux – gouts of astonished blood
in cyan and magenta round the scaffold
of my bones, my meat and my dark caverns? Who's to say
these creamy glands, two butter beans in sanguine sauce,
these devilled kidneys, dark as plums, my lover's liver
glistening like a deepsea conch, this duodenum,
crinkled, damp and pocketed as purple wrack
or the twin seaslugs of my lungs that plunder air
are lovelier or more temperate than another girl's?

Skin-deep's more legible. So now let me enhance
the parts that, underneath this skin, are less than taut
and translate nature's failings with synthetic sympathy
building a shrine in silicone to my elastic youth.
When they stumble on my longbarrow and dig me up,
they'll find my parchment in a randomness of sticks,
my bowl of skull, fissured with fine occiput craquelure,
two black stare-holes. My gaptooth grin. Tangled
in the nuggets of my vertebrae Mum's locket
and on the birdcage of my ribs will sit two jellyfish,
pristine, intact, pert as the day they were slipped in.

CLAUDIA DAVENTRY

The Doll's House

Welcome to my second boudoir, my salon,
    my little beauty parlour
        La Petite Maison –
        you'll know it by the paper lantern
    hanging over the door
and its constant stream of gorgeous women.

Not one of the backstreets' *scalpel and slab*.
    My credentials are good,
        leaving you fresh and pampered –
        not mangled, crisped and toasted,
    broke and left for dead!
I only deal in butterflies and swans.

Give me, let's say, the most unsymmetrical woman –
    I'll make her a Helen of Troy,
        turn a dog's slop-dinner
        into a red hot stunner
    in only half a day.
No hocus pocus – just the Art of Grooming.

I'm trained by a woman who only used her fingers,
    cloth and mirror – nothing more –
        no creams, colours or potions.
        I was hooked, got my own notions,
    took it from there.
Although successful she'd call me a swindler.

Mistress-Madeline of a thousand hairdos,
    the endless counter of creams,
        sticks, polish, soap and scents –
        just watch me turn cracked stumps
    into ruby red talons! –
coax life into a face as grey as mothballs.

I love a challenge and you're getting the best
    at rates that are reasonable.
        My grotto's very well equipped
        to handle any hag or misfit
    and I'll take control.
Trust my experience and impeccable taste.

I'm a devil-good hairdresser – curls or frizz,
    setting it straight or using a colour.
        What you don't want cut or plucked
        I'll coif into a masterpiece!
    I even do cunt-hair
and you should see my collection of antique wigs.

Sample my range of little special somethings
    for anyone and everyone –
        tried and tested treats and peps
        for tired eyes and thinning lips,
    wrinkles, crow's feet, sagging skin.
I'll razor out corns and cold cream bunions.

Throw out your arm, thigh or ankle
    for something more permanent –
        a dainty tattoo (fine ink
        or pig's blood needled under the skin)
    or what about a little ornament –
sparkling jewel to squeeze inside your navel!

Never less than seeking out perfection.
    Similar to an architect,
        ingenious creativity
        and steady hands are necessary.
    One false step
an angel's become a slop-faced slattern.

I swear the world's a sumptuous exhibition
    on a massive stage –
        piece of vaudeville or theatre,
        parade or brilliant gala
    with a stunning showcase
of a hundred thousand stunning women.

And I'm bored with the talk. Call it what you want –
      grease or war-paint,
            touch-up, non-essential,
            cover-up, superficial,
      a bunch of evils in the best arrangement –
it's all crap! Enhancing beauty's an art.

CHERYL FOLLON

Achieving the Lotus Gait

In winter, the uphill path to Madame Xing's
is treacherous. I watch for loose
stones among the grey-brown gravel

and the birds are almost silent
as each step quarries me,
wincing on wooden pattens.

Madame unravels yards of stinking cotton
from my feet and her thorough thumbs
knead them from numbness.

She honours my feet with warmed water,
loosening shedding skin,
trims each bruised nail to the quick.

She rebinds each foot in cotton lengths
soaked in herbs and animal blood.
A neat figure-of-eight turns

over instep, gathers toes, under foot
and round the heel, each pass tighter
than the last. And then my thoughts

cringe homewards, as I totter out under
a brittle moon; my own weight
crushing each foot into the correct shape.

BARBARA SMITH

Recipe for a Saint

Conviction like a gun magazine, youth,
laserbeam eyes, elation, a hymen,
a white robe and a heart that sears the chest.

Around twelve is best, though if the years
have screeched past like demons
in T-birds, not to fret.

Sometimes rapture comes quietly.
Should they be shy on jubilance,
diligence will do.

If you haven't got a virgin, use a penitent.
See Mary M, Mary of Egypt, in fact,
all the bad Marys and a Margaret besides.

The robe is disposable. Indeed
it is usually stripped before execution
and so much the better for tributary paintings.

That heart, strong as a water wheel,
must be saved once removed,
and spirited to the Vatican.

The eyes that lie, gouged and fogging
on the ground, are not so important.
Give them to a child for marbles.

KIRSTEN IRVING

A God-Problem

(FROM *The Theology of Hair*)

Because of my crown, I came to doubt the Word,
and the power of trichologians
to trim it.
They sheared long curls of mortality
with their razors and knives.
'A flock of goats on the mountains of Gilead.'
'Her hair is like unto a mantle of porphyry.'
'If a woman should go bare-headed, she shall be shorn,
and if this step
be distasteful to her, she shall be shaved as well.'
Should a woman be dragged by her hair to a fold
as a lamb to the slaughter? By shepherds? Were they bald?

Standing before your altar,
in my worst nightmares, I see
a woman, shorn, being drowned as a witch,
each single hair plucked out;
another girl reaches out to her,
she is tarred and feathered in dark stains;
she turns into Esther, offers shit and mud
instead of rare perfumes.

Jesus, what would you say today
to women who wear veils?
Is there a place for us in your sanctum?

We long to hear that story
again and again. The one about a sinner.
You let her dry your feet
with the unfettered beauty of her hair
and nobody stopped her. Nobody.

MENNA ELFYN

translated from the Welsh by Elin ap Hywel

Pamela Asks the Right Questions

Pamela had not been a prostitute for long
before her exes wanted to become her clients.
Suddenly, her old boyfriends loved
her body the way children love
strange flowers: raised above a garden's
dirt-bed they wonder what it takes
to be a bee, wonder what it takes
to pluck the stem and drink
the flower's nectar.
Pamela feared that she was
a flower to which the bees only came
for answers. *What answers?*
Pamela wondered out loud
one night when her ex-college-boyfriend Chad
had her lying on her back. *What answers?*
Chad didn't answer,
but she didn't expect him to.
A drop of sweat dripped down
Pamela's cheek.
Her feet gripped the sheets
with their small fingers.
She pictured herself as Eve,
fruit-eaten, waiting hours
for a verdict from God.
In the dark garden, she cloaked herself gently
in palm, pursed her lips, let one
breast fall, as if to plea,
Your godliness, give it to me.
Give me an answer.

KATIE CONDON

The Bed

This is the bed
that I became a woman in,
that I lay naked on on tepid nights,
after my grandmother's scaly-fingered gardener
half-marched, half crept in here and mended it
(like a man mends a cage in a zoo,
with excited reluctance);
I lay in the shade
of this lop-sided wardrobe –
that looks like a caramelised ungainly antelope
with nothing between its head and the constellations
except the occasional stiff-winged aeroplane –

and sent my long gold clitoris to sea
between my legs, streamlined and sweet
like a barge
laden with sweetmeats and monkeys
bound for some distant land;
and this is the bed I saw the chickens from,
running across the yard without their heads,
and smelt the farmers
leaning on their cows that had cars' names –
a smell of blood and milking and desire
I was suddenly part of, and sunk in,
like necks in Startena.

SELIMA HILL

To the vagina

Every poet, drunken fool
Thinks he's just the king of cool,
(Every one is such a boor,
He makes me sick, I'm so demure),

129

He always declaims fruitless praise
Of all the girls in his male gaze.
He's at it all day long, by God,
Omitting the best bit, silly sod:
He praises the hair, gown of fine love,
And all the girl's bits up above,
Even lower down he praises merrily
The eyes which glance so sexily;
Daring more, he extols the lovely shape
Of the soft breasts which leave him all agape,
And the beauty's arms, bright drape,
Even her perfect hands do not escape.
Then with his finest magic
Before night falls, it's tragic,
He pays homage to God's might,
An empty eulogy: it's not quite right:
For he's left the girl's middle unpraised,
That place where children are upraised,
The warm bright quim he does not sing,
That tender, plump, pulsating broken ring,
That's the place I love, the place I bless,
The hidden quim below the dress.
You female body, you're strong and fair,
A faultless, fleshy court plumed with hair.
I proclaim that the quim is fine,
Circle of broad-edged lips divine,
It's a valley, longer than a spoon or hand,
A cwm to hold a penis strong and grand;
A vagina there by the swelling bum,
Two lines of red to song must come.
And the churchmen all, the radiant saints,
When they get the chance, have no restraints,
They never fail their chance to steal,
By Saint Beuno, to give it a good feel.
So I hope you feel well and truly told off,
All you proud male poets, you dare not scoff,
Let songs to the quim grow and thrive
Find their due reward and survive.
For it is silky soft, the sultan of an ode,
A little seam, a curtain on a hole bestowed,

Neat flaps in a place of meeting,
The sour grove, circle of greeting,
Superb forest, faultless gift to squeeze,
Fur for a fine pair of balls, tender frieze,
A girl's thick glade, it is full of love,
Lovely bush, blessed be it by God above.

GWERFUL MECHAIN (1462-1500)
translated from the Welsh by Katie Gramich

Cunt Artist Boyfriend

He told her, keep it neat and tidy.
She thinks, same as the kitchen,
same as the kitchen sink.

She asked how he'd like her done;
a Brazilian, a Hollywood… he said
just keep it neat and tidy.

She combines Brazilian and basic bikini,
it's a shame then that she leaves wet sponges
damply lining the kitchen sink.

He wishes she would wring them out
or not stack used pots to stink like drains,
but leave it neat and tidy, nightly.

It is hard to negotiate hands on flesh
and hard not to complain when cleanliness
comes to grief in the kitchen sink.

Day in and out the chores remain,
monthly hair waxes and wanes.
He congratulates her, you've kept it tidy
all but the kitchen sink.

REBECCA SMITH

the trials and tribulations of a well-endowed woman

my breasts offend my father
even more than my opinions;
it's the size that's insolent – bursting
out of t-shirts, spilling
out of kameezes that hang
demurely on any other girl.

the most mundane actions inspire a filial
mistrust that extends well beyond your
garden-variety middle-class moral suspicion:
going out for coffee with a friend, being on the phone;
in our lounge, leaning back
dupatta-less on the couch becomes
an act of sexual rebellion.
my sisters get hugs;
I, at best, get awkward back-pats.

felt up by a darzi at 10, groped by a driver at 11,
and too many times to count since; intrusive
hands years of poor posture couldn't deflect.
I envy other women their ability to wear
their sexuality like a mask, to take
off and put on as they please
and, not least, I envy them
their delicates that actually
look delicate; mine, all hefty
cotton and industrial-strength
underwire, look just like armour.

fortunately, though, the man I love
loves warriors.

HIRA A.

Across the street

Naailah feeds her newborn son,
at the front of her pink house, sitting
on a wicker chair with yellow cushions
surrounded by purple daisies.

She sings like a brown honeybird
chirping on a beehive. African men
wander by, smile at mother and child,
a few stop to greet the *mama mayo*.

How she would laugh, if I said
a breast was a private part. She'd feel
my forehead, advise against chewing
datura leaves, walking in the midday sun.

Flying home, holding my son close,
I try to feel her presence, hear her laugh
as I hide myself under a smothering blanket,
shamed by a white man in a grey suit.

EVELINE PYE

Kinky Hair Blues

Gwine find a beauty shop
Cause I ain't a belle.
Gwine find a beauty shop
Cause I ain't a lovely belle.
The boys pass me by,
They say I's not so swell.

See oder young gals
So slick and smart.
See dose oder young gals
So slick and smart.
I jes gwine die on de shelf
If I don't mek a start.

I hate dat ironed hair
And dat bleaching skin.
Hate dat ironed hair
And dat bleaching skin.
But I'll be all alone
If I don't fall in.

Lord 'tis you did gie me
All dis kinky hair.
'Tis you did gie me
All dis kinky hair,
And I don't envy gals
What got dose locks so fair.

I like me black face
And me kinky hair.
I like me black face
And me kinky hair.
But nobody loves dem,
I jes don't tink it's fair.

Now I's gwine press me hair
And bleach me skin.
I's gwine press me hair
And bleach me skin.
What won't a gal do
Some kind a man to win.

UNA MARSON

Hollywood Biltmore Hotel

After the guys had got their awards
we understood each other's need
to sag back in our seats
and breathe out.

The matching of ties, tuxedos,
cufflinks, shoes, belts, haircuts
and moustachios
had all been worth it –

for there they were, up on the stage
holding their crystal balls.
A woman beside me leaned in to whisper:
I just want to say how natural you look.

ELAINE BECKETT

Women's Blood

Burn the soiled ones in the boiler,
my mother told me, showing me how to hook
the loops of gauze-covered wadding pads
onto an elastic belt, remembering
how my grandmother had given her
strips of rag she'd had to wash out
every month for herself: the grandmother
who had her chair by the boiler,
who I loved but was plotting to murder
before she murdered my mother, or my mother –
shaking, sobbing, hurling plates and cups,
screaming she wished she'd never been born,
screeching 'Devil!' and 'Witch!' –
murdered her. I piled up the pads
until the smell satisfied me

it was the smell of a corpse.
'How could you do such a thing?'
my mother asked, finding them
at the bottom of the wardrobe
where the year before she'd found
a cache of navy-blue knickers
stained with the black jelly clots
I thought were my wickedness
oozing out of me.

VICKI FEAVER

Cherry Blossoms

Barefoot, I walk to the hen house,
lift the door – reach
into a sanctuary of straw,
find the egg warm
in the cup of my hand.

The new hen still cuckling,
I drop the egg into a pot of water,
butter toast, measure time.

Everything stops as I eat,
my stale thoughts and musty breath,

and I remember
Ellie Byrne and me
looking up through cherry blossoms
at stars and the young night,

our warm round bellies,
before the eggs
began to fall.

LANI O'HANLON

Stained

We're bare-legged and hard-mouthed
our lips slicked hawberry red.
We bleed, stuff wads of cotton inside,
miss swimming because we are 'on'.

We aren't unnerved
when a tampon blooms
in a murky puddle. We let boys
pull us in nodding white cars.

We know how you're made,
how the chalky marks on sheets
get there. You despise us,
yell 'Dirty! Dirty!' and run.

You're not fast.
We pin you down
in briars, stain you,
tell you everything.

HANNAH BROCKBANK

Petals

Better to be fashioned by the weather,
Scouted by insects and
Laced with web,
Than a tamed blossom
Away from wild friends,
A rootless beauty
Garnishing glass.

DONNA BECK

Blood

Indian girls started their periods
earlier, according to my mother.
(I thought that's what she said.)
And she mentioned Neema
who, visiting years before,
one solemn afternoon,
had sat by the rockery
and named her doll after me.
A graceful, ladylike girl, but
suffering early that unimaginable
drip onto something like a dressing,
known by its initials, worn
mysteriously between the legs.
Was I more Indian or more English?
I blurred, as I would forever
when my blood seeped regularly
into the outer world.
I'd even run with that strangeness,
awkward in the egg-and-spoon race,
or guard it in the struggle to pass
an orange hugged under the chin,
hands secured behind my back.

MONIZA ALVI

Down There

The vagina was known, though I couldn't find mine.
In class it was all black lines and cross sections –
below the uterus with its monster arms of fallopian tubes
yah boo-ing back at our 12 year old selves.
It meant periods and sex. Babies if you weren't good.

138

But that other thing – the thing I thought I'd found –
wasn't there, not even in marks on the girls' lavvy wall.
A tiny bud folded in wet silk – I'd fingered it now
and then in the doll-dark of my slippery bed.
It had no name. Perhaps did not exist.

In '70, in case, we went on the pill. Spotty boys,
wearing cheesecloth and hair on its way to long,
made jokes about tunnels, lighthouses, Cadbury's Flake.
But in his room, among the Rizlas and progressive rock,
we just rubbed and fumbled in the dark.

And then, the sweet surprise – like jumping,
trusting myself to air, riding currents off a cliff edge.
I didn't know, and it wasn't like sneezing, and it was sex,
but not *that* sex, lifting me off to a different place.
The thing was a she, and later, strangely Greek or Latinate.

SALLY GOLDSMITH

Horses Sally or Ivy Blue

So come on Lady – how do you like it?
    What are the women saying?
        How do I do it just right?
        Well – keep the pressure on
    but not too *too* much –
like something's squatting between there.

Like something's nosing past the folds of a –
    well, a lady's dress –
        a really big heavy rich one,
        you know, heavy as hell
    and rich as a rose.
Do you get me? Or nudging past silk.

And what about the tongue? O sweet one
    that's the easy part.
        Couple it up with little sucks –
        and not too much attack –
    like you're chasing a lone pea
inside a – jug of – milk – with your tongue!

Do you want me to stick a finger in?
    Is that what you want?
        If that's what you really fancy
        then two or three are dandy.
    And just like the mouth.
Just like you're kissing me on the mouth.

Someone might like it seven inches in
    and another light as a pin.
        But nothing too paddle-like,
        or like some great woofer
    sucking marrow out a bone.
Come on. Get to work you son-of-a-whore.

CHERYL FOLLON

Fanny Farts

To the dear American, fanny fart might
mean a bottom burp. But this ain't what I mean.
Keister ain't the place I intend to pour praise.
        It's more the quim quake.

Pressure builds as squelchiness seals escape. Plunge
lavish length in, burial deep inside, slide
back and forth, the vacuum effect to cause post
        coital cunt cough.

140

During lunging, pockets of air get stuck till
he withdraws and gurgling noises trumpet,
like the Eastern custom to belch a full meal,
                    forced by a tight fit.

Girls' regard for girth can applaud with muff guff.
Gorging gusset sounding the pussy parp stress.
Thunderclap the wonderful width; the whole hole's
                    rippling fanfare.

Bodies all have ways to express excess wind.
Whoopee cushion winkles are loud and clear, mere
suction function ain't to be blushing beetroot;
                    welcome the size prize.

SUE SPIERS

Jardi d'Eros, Barcelona

At the exhibition of erotic art
I see more than I expected –
take penises, for instance –
how, *en masse*,
they lose most of their appeal,
their potency
and that veiled threat
even the best of them offer
and how instead
they become innocent,
mild and sweet
as mushrooms in a field
or like pallid sea-anemones
swaying gently to and fro
whereas female pudenda,
usually so docile,

so inviting
with their pretty ways
and sleek little curls –
they take courage in a crowd,
gang up and, if pushed,
turn nasty, snapping
at men who peer too closely,
making them tremble.

ANGELA KIRBY

For the Punters

You don't see them, only hear their clatter, mutter, snigger,
then the whoop when you come on, the urge and whistle
to *get on with it*, go *all the way*. And I go slowly
all the way each night, right there into the glare
of the spot, the glamour-light that turns dust into glitter.

One night I'd like to stop it there, rewind the routine music
and begin again from naked – strip my skin off, peel it down
my shoulders, arms and chest, past waist and hips, unravel it
down either leg, step out, then screw it up and fling it.

Then I'd ease off my flesh and be a bone woman,
they'd see me phosphorescent in the stagelight, dancing
like a puppet jerked on strings, and in the dumbstruck quiet
they'd hear me hiss and cackle, whistle back at them.

SUSAN UTTING

Trinity

I

Once there was a woman with a big mouth.

She opened it wide in hunger.
She opened it wide in anger.
She opened it wide in laughter.

Her mouth was so wide that when she was hungry,
she could eat you whole.

Her mouth was so wide that when she was angry,
lightning sparked from her throat.

Her mouth was so wide that when she laughed,
the whole earth shook.

One day when she'd had enough of the world,
she opened her big mouth & swallowed it
& kept it quietly inside her.

II

Once there was a woman who grew hair on her face.
She didn't grow it to make people snigger behind their hands
& she didn't grow it to make a point.

When her friends took her aside to talk discreetly about
depilatory creams & electrolysis
she just smiled a smile of serenity & grew her hair a little longer
(soft hair, womanly hair).

She didn't grow it so people would stare at her in the street
& she didn't grow it so they'd turn away from her in lifts.

& when small children tugged at their fathers' hands & said
'Look Daddy, that lady's got a beard!'
she just smiled a little smile inside, all to herself
& grew her hair just that much thicker
(lustrous hair, feminine hair).

So that the hair on her face grew & grew
all soft & curly & growing
until it developed into a dense, tangled thicket
& Piwakawaka the fantail came to live in it
& sang sweetly in her ear.

III

Once there was a woman who asked the Great Goddess:
What shall become of me?

And the Immense Goddess spoke to her
in her huge roaring voice saying:
You will have many husbands
& several wives
(not all at once, necessarily)
because I have chosen you
you who are a great lump of onyx among women
to go forth and, well,
not exactly multiply with all these folk,
but at least have a very jolly time of it.

Lay hold of the Tree of Life, said the Enormous Goddess
(oh yea) and sip at the Endless Well.
You go for it, she said.
Go get 'em.

Thus the woman knew she had been sanctified
& that is why she recommends
you just open your heart as wide as it goes
& damn well enjoy yourself.

JANIS FREEGARD

Happiness

My hair is happy
and my skin is happy.
My skin quivers with happiness.

I breathe happiness instead of air,
slowly and deeply,
as a man who avoided a mortal danger.

Tears roll down my face,
I do not know it.
I forget I still have a face.
My skin is singing,
I shiver.

I feel time's duration
as it felt in the hour of death.
As if my sense of time alone were grasping the world,
as if existence were time only.
Immersed in terrifying
magnificence
I feel every second of happiness, as it arrives,
fills up, bursts into flower
according to its own natural way,
unhurried as a fruit,
astounding as a deity.

Now
I begin to scream.
I am screaming. I leave my body.
I do not know whether I am human anymore,
how could anyone know that, screaming with happiness.
Yet one dies from such screaming,
thus I am dying from happiness.
On my face there are probably no more tears,
my skin probably does not sing by now.
I don't know whether I still have a skin,
from me to my skin
is too far to know.

Soon I will go.
I do not shiver any longer,
I do not breathe any longer.
I don't know whether I still have
something to breathe with.

I feel time's duration,
how perfectly I feel time's duration.

I sink
I sink into time.

ANNA SWIR
translated by Czesław Miłosz & Leonard Nathan

Could it be

When you leave
I smiling hold
this soft furry
bouncing
tingling
tickling
I don't know what to call it
'thing'

it moves round me
all day
moves me round
all day

tickling tingly 'thing'

waiting to bounce out
my eyes
my mouth

my ears
my nose
my belly
my thighs
and all those other shy soft places
waiting to be named
in subtler tones

waiting to bounce out
soft funny
bouncy cuddly
tingling tickly
ah! so touchy tender 'thing'
waiting to bounce out at you
when you get home

could it be.

JEAN 'BINTA' BREEZE

My Black Triangle

My black triangle
sandwiched between the geography of my thighs

is a bermuda
of tiny atoms
forever seizing
and releasing
the world

My black triangle
is so rich
that it flows over
on to the dry crotch
of the world

My black triangle
is black light
sitting on the threshold of the world
overlooking
all my probabilities

And though
it spares a thought for history
my black triangle
has spread beyond his story
beyond the dry fears of parch-ri-archy

Spreading and growing
trusting and flowing
my black triangle
carries the seal of approval
of my deepest self.

Reading My Skin

You read me as if I were braille
your fingertips move over each of my limbs.
On my left thigh you touch *sad*, on my right
lonely, where your pinky presses down
as if to double-check. I feel you
search for other words.

You stroke the inside of my legs,
find *broken*, then travel to my belly, pause
at *Bolivia* and *English*, confused
and it's not till they touch *perdida*
that they begin to understand my unease
while you read me. On my feet's soles,
where the skin is hard, you find *fall*, *Tarija*
near the number *four*.

At my knees *Huntsville, Texas* where
you stop for five seconds, tapping on *strangers,*
religion and *home* where I try to nudge
your fingers away but still you look
for other codes and find only
scattered question marks.

But you pause longer, almost a minute
at my hip bone, on *New York, Joe, John*
and a word even you won't say aloud
and begin to realise why
I was reluctant to be read.
You stop on my left breast at *Edinburgh*
and *tha gaol agam ort*, not wanting
or needing to feel anymore.

KATHERINE LOCKTON

Full-length Mirror

Sally the therapist stops by on Mondays.
Bright and brunette, she accepts, smiling,
the snail and bag of screws Billy gifts her,
then sets them down like the Turin Shroud
and chats to Matron, before going up.

I share with Medusa, so sometimes
I wander in during their sessions,
pretending not to listen. Thought
I was in love when I saw her unpacking.
Shy, huge eyes and a full-on kapow
of a body. But we're all nuts here.

Sally asks about the zoo, the food,
stays safe to build rapport. Gets grunts.
Medusa pretends to read, her oilslick hair
pooling on the pages of *Jane Eyre*.

Sally asks if it's a good book.
Medusa doesn't look up.
The therapist hefts a full-length mirror
across; asks if they could both glance
into it together.

The second night, I crept into her covers,
murmuring compliments, trying to sneak
a kiss, my tongue like a cobra; a finger.
The doctor, stitching stoicly,
said I was lucky.

I gather what I say I came in for
and turn to go as they both stand up,
shrink and shrinkee, to face the glass.

Medusa shrugs and says she feels
the same as ever –
she wants her head cut off.

Sally nods, Sally sighs a century.

KIRSTEN IRVING

On Nudity

The moon sits in the sky
like that stray cat sits in my window.

The cat stares at me & because I don't feel
dirty enough I walk outside & knead

my fingers into its flea filled neck.
I see my neighbour naked at her counter,

moonlight tattooed to her nape & I think,
I need to go the gym.

I need to stand naked at my counter
so I can leave the blinds up & be

objectified by my neighbours & the moon.
I usually mind my own business, but smile

when my neighbour turns around slightly
horrified. The stray arches its back

into a soft crescent against my hand,
against the darkness of a siren shrieking

into a hospital's empty bay.

KATIE CONDON

I Think of You and Think of Skin

I think of you and think of skin –
its soft stretch, ways it may fold, or be pressed,
occasionally tear. How it absorbs the fix it's in,
ends up not innocent, unkissed, yet simple in its rest –

your father's work, to expose such by the sun,
harried and tawed and dressed for the intent
of its disguise with musks and roses. For you, years gone,
I'm pale now, peeled, unwritten-on, a reproach unmeant –

white widow in my quilled intransigence, a swan
alone. Days such as these, late summer of my life,
I wonder at this want to turn a yearling's tongue
to subtleties so hollow, telling tender lies –

those nights you travelled me with words, blood-nibbed
and burning, tell me I was your first, flawed, outlawed script.

PIPPA LITTLE

John Shakespeare, William's father, was a 'whyttawer' (worker in white leather) who made gloves from calf, kid, lamb and rabbit skins so fine they were almost translucent. He might spend up to a year preparing the hides before beginning his work. The sonnet is in Anne Hathaway's voice. [PL]

No, Mon Amour

My breast
(the right one)
shrinks inside its pouch.
It is pale,
toadhearted.
The lesser breast
suffers the most.
Poor relative
of the breast with the franchise,
specially commissioned theme tune
and gift shop.
How often people presume
that the agony of the breasts
is double!
No, mon amour.
While the left
is crushed and petted,
the orphan right
silently hungers.
The animal slopes
back to its room.
If only the scenario
weren't so
laughable.
If only the left
didn't swell
with each hard twist
of the nipple.

AMY McCAULEY

God Save me from women with Choppy Bobs

Who sashay into the office wearing too much fake-tan
and talk about gastric bands, crow's feet, cracked heels.

They all eat sushi and talk about their clitoris every seven seconds
and swish their hair like Claudia Schiffer and tweet minor celebs
and wonder what they would do if they ever got stretch marks
and they once made a suicide pact in the conference suite.
Kill me if my breasts ever sag or if I get so fat that men
no longer find me attractive, even my husband they say.

Darling I'm wearing Eau de parfum by Katie Price.
Can you smell the long top notes of dewy lime? they ask

before inviting each other to run their fingers along
the smoothness of their product perfect skin
but these women fall silent
whenever I enter the room
then they eek amongst themselves like mice.

What does it feel like to be youngish and only have one breast? they ask.

I could try to explain it differs from woman to woman.
I could say quite honestly to me it doesn't matter
that having one breast makes me unique
actually, it makes me feel like an amazon queen.

Save me from these women.

I know the world can't be full of women with cropped, black hair
who won't give themselves to the darkness no matter what.

But all the same God save me.

NICOLA DALY

Sexted

It happened at school, in Drama: some girl
sent photos to a guy who sent them to another guy
who got off the hook. Apparently there's a line
and if you cross it you're an on-site lifeguard,
the rest of us quietly drowning until we're saved.
She managed to cry in the right scene, but it wasn't
about the play. She shook for days. Like his phone
when he got the text, dropped like a bomb
in his pocket. We looked at the floor and the fates
spun in the corridors. She left the stage. Those of us
who've been there and lived, we didn't dare say.
After all, why try to explain what nobody saw:
that somebody somewhere must have looked at her
full-on, too hard too long, set her in freefall.

JASMINE SIMMS

Not Andromeda

I cannot hang damselled in the night sky for you –
        lunar, the translucent lilt
      of alabaster skin, slender arms,
     fingers which taper to vanishing points
    and, like hot glass, slowly fold into place,
   sitting quietly. I cannot grow legs which
  slide, waxen, down your glance
 with tiny feet bound
to a pulp and my bones
do not quiver with fear
in egg shell threads, stitched together
in a diminuendo of the waist and a fine needlework
of the voice.

I cannot be Andromeda.
As a mortal I do not require your worship, nor your

offerings at my feet to guarantee you
a rich harvest. The corners of your plinth bruise
my dappling of cellulite, pomegranate
flesh, clay left
with the impressions of
a creator's thumbs. I possess
a body full and strong, folding like an artery
or a root feasting, sunk in earth – rough, furrowed,
rashed with lichen.

If I am celestial at all, it is because
                    we were both drawn
          from the same flaming blood, a light shed
from the first sighs of the stars.

Let us grasp each other's shoulders.
Let us share a look of understanding.
Let me be a brother to you, even though
I am not a man.

KATIE BYFORD

The Blossom Queen

She is a waif.
Her petal skin peels away
To the safe-lock of her budding heart.

She is brief.
Making way for fruits sweeter
And flesh firmer
Than her own supple limbs.

Green eyes gaze.
New life gasps inside her.
The confetti at her wedding was death.

LORNA SCOTT

How to Make Love Not Like a Porn Star

Teach me to make love not like a porn star,
make me a bed that has nothing to prove. Let's laugh
at unscripted noises; let's not care what it looks like.
Persuade my body to forget what it knows.
Let me breathe in and out to the fit of your hands.
Let me let myself not always be camera ready.
Show me a picture of me not doing a Marilyn Monroe.
Let me see that your eyes are not apertures.
Let's sink to cliché, let your eyes be rock pools
I hitch up my skirt and wade in, reach down to return
dirty finger-nailed, with a fistful of small shiny stones.
Teach me to close my eyes without making them.
Teach me to expect no result, zoom in for no reason
on the cleavage of your chin my pinkie fits in.
Let us not talk about the size of anything.
Teach me to listen, find a gasp in your hello,
how you make it sound like the first line in a tall tale.
Let your tongue be a silver river. Teach me to sail.
Let there be hair. Let's mention things that aren't hard.
Let my breasts look unlikely in your fisherman's hands,
the blisters and scars like snow globes I find myself in.
Let us wake with limbs tangled as Chinese puzzles,
and garlic bread by the bed. Open your eyes, lashes
like footprints of snow-laden birds; let me pull off the sleep.

ANGELA READMAN

homage to my hips

these hips are big hips
they need space to
move around in.
they don't fit into little

156

petty places. these hips
are free hips.
they don't like to be held back.
these hips have never been enslaved,
they go where they want to go
they do what they want to do.
these hips are mighty hips.
these hips are magic hips.
i have known them
to put a spell on a man and
spin him like a top!

LUCILLE CLIFTON

Woman Solstice

On the longest day
head bursting with hidden thunder
I go to find icons.
I am bleeding
bruised red petals,
and thinking of old bones;
new cries.
The sheela-na-gigs
lie in a dank crypt
flanked by ogham stones
and carved shards,
tagged and crumbling.
The sheelas squat on shelves –
forgotten; defiant.
One opens her legs
in a glaze of red,
one mocks death
with a thick glare
and a thrusting tongue.

Another gives herself joy
with a finger
on her pleasure pulse.
Some are featureless,
breastless,
but all open knees
pulling wide labia
with large, insistent hands.

They dare the eye to recoil.

The longest day
throbs to an end
blue light fading slow;
as I watch the roll
of the moon's disc
behind gathering clouds,
I am lying on cool sheets
splay-thighed
and smiling.

KATIE DONOVAN

Descendant

Not from the warm heart
of America or the flatlander folk
our mother recalls
drinking Whiskey Sours
in her parents' Wisconsin garden –
we are of these hornblende hulls,
Pacific, salted, our faces
freckled with quartz, feldspar
and St Helen's ash.
Here there is no long summer.

We are saplings
grown in pine's shadow –
stunted, pale, our nails black
from digging loamy soil.
The vibration of glaciers
passing over granite
echoes in our spines, our skin
is woven from the wet
spore of decay. But I am
feverish from the seep

of magma, choked
by the hot breath of the mantle.
Sister, you must also
smell the sulphur-smoking
crater, hear the lisping
red tongues of tube worms,
feel the slip of the plate
subducting beneath
this fault. Tell me, sister,
you also burn.

KRIS JOHNSON

Professor

In my study of female circumcision
Amongst the Sudanese tribes,
It has been interesting to note
That the procedure has no noticeable effect
On subsequent marriage and childbearing,
And that few side effects trouble the patient.
It's important to know how the women themselves
Champion the practice, or so I gather

When I am able to talk to them,
Which is not often,
Owing to the various tribes' particular codes of conduct
Which I am loathe to break.
However, I have asked them to describe the procedure –
The knife, the needles, the sutures, the aftercare –
Not because I take pleasure
In hearing about such things (needless to say)
But because there isn't the pain you'd expect.
They just go numb

As if the spirits have departed them
To race across the plains,
Trampling the dust of the plains
And disappearing over the edge of the world.

EVA SALZMAN

After Reading *Mickey in the Night Kitchen* for the Third Time Before Bed

I'm in the milk and the milk's in me!.. I'm Mickey!

My daughter spreads her legs
to find her vagina:
hairless, this mistaken
bit of nomenclature
is what a stranger cannot touch
without her yelling. She demands
to see mine and momentarily
we're a lopsided star
among the spilled toys,
my prodigious scallops
exposed to her neat cameo.

And yet the same glazed
tunnel, layered sequences.
She is three; that makes this
innocent. *We're pink!*
she shrieks, and bounds off.

Every month she wants
to know where it hurts
and what the wrinkled string means
between my legs. *This is good blood*
I say, but that's wrong, too.
How to tell her that it's what makes us –
black mother, cream child.
That we're in the pink
and the pink's in us.

RITA DOVE

Bless me Father

for I have loved another,
pressed my body
tight against theirs
until there was no space
left between us,
only the sound of our breaths
moving in unison
like a slow symphony.

Bless me Father
for I have found pleasure
hidden in the old well
and I have drunk from it
until I was giddy,
overcome with delight,
until I wanted to shout

the name of God
from every roof top in Ireland.

Bless me Father
for I have fought
with your rules
on the bloody battle-
ground of my body,
for I had forgotten this song,
buried in the flesh of my soul
like a deep river,
singing through my veins.

Bless me father
for I have sinned;
I have listened
to you and your like
for far too long,
and I have ignored
the quiet voice whispering
between my legs,
exploding through my heart
and blessing me over
and over again.

SIOBHÁN MAC MAHON

I'll Be a Wicked Old Woman

I'll be a wicked old woman
Thin as a rail,
The way I am now.
Not one of those big-assed ones
With buttocks churning behind them,
As Celine said.

Not one of the good-natured grandmas and aunties
Against whose soft and plump arms
It is nice to lay one's cheek.
I'm more like a scarecrow
In our gardens full of rosy tomatoes
Like children's cheeks.
There are some old crones
Who are both vivacious and angry as a bee
With eyes on top of their heads
Who see everything, hear everything and have an opinion –
Grumblers since birth.
I'll squawk and chatter all day,
Cackle like a hen over her chicks
About the days when I was
A young, good-looking girl,
When I led boys by the nose.
Colts and stallions I tamed
With the flash in my eye, the flash of my skirt,
Passing over infidelities and miseries
The way a general passes over his lost battles.
I'll be free to do anything as an old woman,
Among things I still can and want to do
Like playing bridge or dancing
The light-footed dances of my days.
I'll spin and trip on my sticklike legs,
Attached to my body like toothpicks to a kabob.
That old hag sure can boogie!
The young smarties gathered around me
Will shout and applaud.
An old woman like a well-baked bun with sesame seeds,
That's what I'm going to be like.
I'll stick between everyone's teeth, as I did before
While with a wide hat and dresses down to the ground
I stroll through the landscapes of my past life.
Smelling the furze, admiring the heather,
On every thistle catching my undergarment – my soul.

RADMILA LAZIĆ

translated from the Serbian by Charles Simic

to my last period

well girl, goodbye,
after thirty-eight years.
thirty-eight years and you
never arrived
splendid in your red dress
without trouble for me
somewhere, somehow.

now it is done,
and i feel just like
the grandmothers who,
after the hussy has gone,
sit holding her photograph
and sighing, *wasn't she*
beautiful? wasn't she beautiful?

LUCILLE CLIFTON

Hallelujah for 50ft Women

Hallelujah to lasses who got too big for their boots
who stepped outside the fitting rooms of Mother's
eyes, hair cut with razors, pocket tattoos on a breast
that keeps the names of anyone who made it skip
a beat. Look to such a girl strolling home, 50ft tall,
a milkman's light dabbing sequins on her skirt.
You don't have to know if she's going dancing too soon
or skated over the hours you slept. Marvel at one eye
at the flat window, looking in at sunburnt neighbours,
faces pink as the contents of a bubblegum machine.
Feel a woman breathe, all your furniture suddenly paper,
chairs scraping across the dollhouse floor of your world.

She breathes in, breathes out, walks on. Look
to keep up, consider the size of the act of her crushing
no one, carefully side-stepping policemen, helmets
glinting bottle caps, megaphones like wasps.
There is no weapon she drops, you see the only
weapon she has is herself, one finger trailing along
the frosted roofs of hotels concrete statues
like wedding cakes left out for the birds. Put faith
in the smallness of yourself, sweat by the river
as she slips off her shoes, cools a foot in the water
outside the opera house – a mirror of sky and skyfancying girls.
Look to the seagulls coasting on waves her toes
dip and dab, attempt to sing her praises without a tune,
envy them. Be afraid, one move can kill us, call her name.
Let us be ants on her palm, lifted, lifted to meet her eye.

ANGELA READMAN

On seeing the Furies in the sky

For all the world like a trio of wild-haired women
breasting out of that cloud – the prows of three ships
arms outstretched behind them, coasting the blue.

And why less real than this sunshine
back-lighting my garden, the halo
around the hedge, the green plastic chair

that holds my dreamlike limbs
– as unconnected to me as those three
on their way to vengeance against, please…

the summertime whine
of next door's boys, desperate to cry out,
and their hammering father.

One of them soon will raise
the first fist, the 'not fair' hymn
to the ignored mother I can hear

saying to no one listening,
no one at all but me, saying 'look,
look at those women up there, riding the day'.

HEIDI WILLIAMSON

Deaths of Flowers

I would if I could choose
Age and die outwards as a tulip does;
Not as this iris drawing in, in-coiling
Its complex strange taut inflorescence, willing
Itself a bud again – though all achieved is
No more than a clenched sadness,

The tears of gum not flowing.
I would choose the tulip's reckless way of going;
Whose petals answer light, altering by fractions
From closed to wide, from one through many perfections,
Till wrecked, flamboyant, strayed beyond recall,
Like flakes of fire they piecemeal fall.

E.J. SCOVELL

ACKNOWLEDGEMENTS

Previously published poems in this anthology are reprinted from the following books, all by permission of the publishers listed unless stated otherwise, or from the magazines or websites noted below. Thanks are due to all the copyright holders cited for their kind permission:

Hira A.: 'The trials and tribulations of a well-endowed woman' from *The Missing Slate* (themissingslate.com), by permission of the author. **Kim Addonizio**: 'What Do Women Want?' from *Tell Me*, copyright © 2000 by Kim Addonizio, reprinted with the permission of The Permissions Company, Inc., on behalf of BOA Editions, Ltd, www.boaeditions.org; this poem is also published in *Wild Nights: New & Selected Poems* (Bloodaxe Books, 2015). **Moniza Alvi**: 'Picnic' and 'Blood' from *Split World: Poems 1990-2005* (Bloodaxe Books, 2008).

Mary Barber: 'Stella and Flavia', from *Eliza's Babes: four centuries of women's poetry in English, c. 1500-1900*, ed. Robyn Bolam (Bloodaxe Books, 2005). **Sujata Bhatt**: *Collected Poems* (Carcanet Press, 2013). **Ana Blandiana**: *The Cricket's Eye* (1981), translation by Paul Scott Derrick and Viorica Patea first published in this anthology. **Jean 'Binta' Breeze**: 'Could it be' from *Third World Girl: Selected Poems*, with live DVD (Bloodaxe Books, 2011). **Zoë Brigley**: 'Infertility' from *Conquest* (Bloodaxe Books, 2012); 'The Shave', previously unpublished.

Kimberly Campanello: 'The Green' from *Consent* (Doire Press, 2013). **Kate Clanchy**: 'Miscarriage, Midwinter', from *Selected Poems* (Picador, 2014), by permission of Macmillan Publishers Ltd. **Lucille Clifton**: 'homage to my hips' and 'to my last period' from *The Collected Poems of Lucille Clifton*, copyright © 1991 by Lucille Clifton, reprinted with the permission of The Permissions Company, Inc. on behalf of BOA Editions Ltd, www.boaeditions.org. **Anna Crowe**: 'Trunk of fig tree from Ses Rossells' from *The Figure in the Landscape* (Mariscat Press, 2010) by permission of the author.

Imtiaz Dharker: 'Honour killing' from *I Speak for the Devil* (Bloodaxe Books, 2001). **Katie Donovan**: 'Underneath Our Skirts' and 'Winter Soltice' from *Rootling: New & Selected Poems* (Bloodaxe Books, 2010). **Tishani Doshi**: 'The Magic of the Foot' from

Everything Begins Elsewhere (Bloodaxe Books, 2014). **Rita Dove:** 'After Reading Mickey *in the Night Kitchen* for the Third Time Before Bed', from *Grace Notes* (W.W. Norton, 1989), copyright © 1989 by Rita Dove, by permission of the author and W.W. Norton & Company, Inc. **Carol Ann Duffy:** 'Recognition' from *New Selected Poems* (Picador, 2009), by permission of Macmillan Publishers Ltd. **Helen Dunmore:** 'Three Ways of Recovering a Body' from *Out of the Blue: Poems 1975-2001* (Bloodaxe Books, 2001).

Menna Elfyn: 'A God-Problem', tr. Elin ap Hywel, from *Perfect Blemish: New & Selected Poems 1995-2007 / Perffaith Nam: Dau Ddetholiad & Cherddi Newydd 1995-2007* (Bloodaxe Books, 2007). **Eliza:** 'To a Friend for Her Naked Breasts', from *Eliza's Babes: four centuries of women's poetry in English, c. 1500-1900*, ed. Robyn Bolam (Bloodaxe Books, 2005). **Rebecca Elson:** 'Antidote to the Fear of Death' from *Responsibility to Awe* (Carcanet Press, 2001).

Vicki Feaver: 'Women's Blood' from *The Handless Maiden* (Jonathan Cape, 1994); 'The Woman Who Talked to Her Teeth' from *The Book of Blood* (Jonathan Cape, 2006), by permission of The Random House Group Limited. **Cheryl Follon:** 'The Doll's House' from *All Your Talk* (Bloodaxe Books, 2004); 'Horse Sally or Ivy Blue' from *Dirty Looks* (Bloodaxe Books, 2010). **Angela France:** 'A Fallow Blooming' from *Occupation* (Ragged Raven Press, 2009) by permission of the author. **Janis Freegard:** 'Trichotillomania' and 'Trinity' from *Kingdom Animalia: The Escapades of Linnaeus* (Auckland University Press, 2011).

Kerry Hammerton: 'On New Year's Eve' from *The Weather Report* (Kerry Hammerton, Cape Town, 2014), by permission of the author. **Kerry Hardie:** 'Flesh' from *Selected Poems* (Bloodaxe Books, UK; Gallery Press, Ireland, 2011), by permission of the author and The Gallery Press, Loughcrew, Oldcastle, Co. Meath, Ireland, www.gallerypress.ie. **Rita Ann Higgins:** 'The Liberator' from *Throw in the Vowels: New & Selected Poems* (Bloodaxe Books, 2005). **Selima Hill:** 'Chocolate' from *Fruitcake* (Bloodaxe Books, 2009); 'The Bed' from *Gloria: Selected Poems* (Bloodaxe Books, 2008).

Kirsten Irving: 'Recipe for a Saint' and 'Full-length Mirror' from *Never, Never, Never Come Back* (Salt Publishing, 2012).

Maria Jastrzębska: 'The Room of Coughing' from *Everyday Angels* (Waterloo Press, 2009).

Jackie Kay: 'Where It Hurts' from *Darling: New & Selected*

Poems (Bloodaxe Books, 2007). **Chris Kinsey:** 'A Clearing' from *Kung Fu Lullabies* (Ragged Raven Press, 2004) by permission of the author. **Angela Kirby:** 'Jardi D'Eros, Barcelona' from *Mr Irresistible* (Shoestring Press, 2005).

Radmila Lazic: 'I'll Be a Wicked Old Woman', tr. Charles Simic, from *A Wake for the Living*, copyright © 1998, 2000, 2001 by Radmila Lazic, translation copyright © 2003 by Charles Simic, by permission of The Permissions Company, Inc. on behalf of Graywolf Press, Minneapolis, Minnesota, www.graywolfpress.org. **Patricia Lockwood:** 'Rape Joke' from *Motherland Fatherland Homelandsexuals*, copyright © by Patricia Lockwood, by permission of Penguin Books, an imprint of Penguin Publishing Group, a division of Penguin Random House LLC.

Amy McCauley: 'No, Mon Amour' first published in *The Stinging Fly*. **Hollie McNish:** 'Embarrassed' from *Nobody Told Me* (Blackfriars Books, 2016), by permission of the author.

Una Marson: 'Kinky Hair Blues' from *The Moth and the Star* (Una Marson, Jamaica, 1937), reprinted in *Modern Women Poets*, ed. Deryn Rees Jones (Bloodaxe Books, 2005), copyright holder not traced. **Gwerful Mechain:** 'To the Vagina', tr. Katie Gramich, from *Welsh Women's Poetry: 1460-2001*, eds. Catherine Brennan and Katie Gramich (Honno, 2003), by permission of the translator. **Sinéad Morrissey:** 'Genetics' from *The State of the Prisons* (Carcanet Press, 2005).

Grace Nichols: 'Invitation' and 'My Black Triangle' from *I Have Crossed an Ocean: Selected Poems* (Bloodaxe Books, 2010), by permission of Curtis Brown Group Ltd, London, on behalf of Grace Nichols, copyright © Grace Nichols, 1984, 2010. **Mary Noonan:** 'Bright Day' from *The Fado House* (Dedalus Press, 2012).

Lani O'Hanlon: 'Cherry Blossoms' first published in *The Stinging Fly*. **Sharon Olds:** 'Self-portrait, Rear View' from *One Secret Thing* (Jonathan Cape, 2009), by permission of The Random House Group Limited. **Leanne O'Sullivan:** 'Bulimia' from *Waiting for My Clothes* (Bloodaxe Books, 2004).

Sally Read: 'Breaking Fish Necks' from *The Point of Splitting* (Bloodaxe Books, 2005). **Janet Rogerson:** 'The Dowry', first published in *The Rialto*, 76 (2012).

Eva Salzman: 'Professor' from *Double Crossing: New & Selected Poems* (Bloodaxe Books, 2004). **Lesley Saunders:** 'In Praise of Footbinding', first published in *The North*, 52 (Spring 2014). **E.J.**

Scovell: 'Deaths of Flowers' from *Collected Poems* (Carcanet Press, 1988). **Warsan Shire:** 'The Ugly Daughter' from *Ten: the new wave* (Bloodaxe Books, 2014), by permission of the author. **Barbara Smith:** 'Pair Bond' and 'Achieving the Lotus Gait' from *The Angel's Share* (Doghouse Books, 2012). **Arundhathi Subramaniam:** 'Rutting' from *Where I Live: New & Selected Poems* (Bloodaxe Books, 2009). **Anna Swir:** 'Happiness' from *Talking to My Body*, translated by Czesław Miłosz and Leonard Nathan, copyright © 1996 by Czesław Miłosz and Leonard Nathan, by permission of The Permissions Company, Inc. on behalf of Copper Canyon Press, www.coppercanyonpress.org. **May Swenson:** 'Question' from *Nature Poems Old and New* (Mariner Books, 1994).

Susana Thénon: 'Nuptial Song', tr. Maria Negroni, first published in *Being Human*, ed. Neil Astley (Bloodaxe Books, 2011), by permission of the translator. **Chase Twichell:** 'Horse' from *Horses Where the Answers Should Have Been: New & Selected Poems* (Bloodaxe Books, UK; Copper Canyon Press, USA, 2010).

Heidi Williamson: 'On seeing the Furies in the sky' from *Electric Shadow* (Bloodaxe Books, 2011). **Anna Woodford:** 'Darling Kisses', first published in *The North*, 46 (2010).

Dimitra Xidous: 'Peach Season' from *Keeping Bees* (Doire Press, 2014).

All other poems were first published in this anthology, and thanks are due to those authors for granting their permission.

Every effort has been made to trace copyright holders of the poems published in this book. The editors and publisher apologise if any material has been included without permission or without the appropriate acknowledgement, and would be glad to be told of anyone who has not been consulted.

INDEX OF POETS

ABOUT RAVING BEAUTIES

Raving Beauties are Sue Jones-Davies, Fan Viner and Dee Orr (and founder member Anna Carteret).

In the Pink, our first cabaret of songs and poetry opened in a pub, sold out at the Edinburgh Festival and featured on Channel 4's opening night in 1982. *Make It Work* was commissioned for Channel 4's second birthday. A third show about the relationship between mothers and daughters, *Tea at the Ritz*, premièred at the Young Vic Studio.

The Women's Press invited us to edit collections of poetry inspired by our shows. This led to *In the Pink* (1983), *No Holds Barred* (1985), an introduction to the work of Anna Swir, *Fat Like the Sun* (1986), and a collection of prose and poetry about relationship breakdown, *Bust Up* (1992).

Raving Beauties have toured their shows in the UK, Ireland, Guernsey, Norway and Spain, and received British Council funding to visit Jamaica and Mexico. Our shows and books which explore issues including work, motherhood, love, creativity, sex and violence have touched the lives of thousands of women. We owe a huge debt of gratitude to the women whose poetry we are still fortunate enough to publish and perform.

Sue Jones-Davies, with a history as a singer and actor spanning many years is probably best known as 'the Welsh tart' in Monty Python's *Life of Brian*. She was a member of the Bowles Brothers Band and the Welsh singing duo Cusan Tan. Sue now spends most of her time teaching yoga and as a forester in Wales.

Dee Orr is an actor, musician and singer whose career began in bands such as Hi Jinx. She has worked extensively in theatre and her many television appearances include Alan Bleasdale's *GBH*. Dee also spent several years as a tutor and healer at The College of Psychic Studies in London.

Fan Viner has acted, directed, written poetry and plays and taught in many different institutions including a prison, universities and a psychiatric hospital. Most recently she has received Arts Council awards for community multimedia performances and installations, a new initiative developed with the De La Warr Pavilion, Bexhill, a contemporary art gallery with an international reputation. She lives in Hastings.

MIX
Paper from
responsible sources
FSC® C007785